THE WASTE LAND

EDITED BY
TONY DAVIES AND
NIGEL WOOD

Learning Resources
Centre

OPEN UNIVERSITY PRESS
BUCKINGHAM · PHILADELPHIA

Open University Press
Celtic Court
22 Ballmoor
Buckingham
MK18 1XW

and

1900 Frost Road, Suite 101
Bristol, PA 19007, USA

First Published 1994

A catalogue record of this book is available from the British Library

ISBN 0 335 15716 5 (pb)

Library of Congress Cataloging-in-Publication Data

The Waste Land / edited by Tony Davies and Nigel Wood.
    p.   cm. — (Theory in practice series)
  Includes bibliographical references and index.
  ISBN 0–335–15716–5
  1. Eliot, T.S. (Thomas Stearns), 1888–1965. Waste land.
I. Davies, Tony, 1940– . II. Wood, Nigel, 1953– . III. Series.
PS3509.L43W3835   1994
811′.52—dc20   93–20998
                                                          CIP

Typeset by Colset Pte Ltd, Singapore
Printed in Great Britain by St Edmundsbury Press,
Bury St Edmunds, Suffolk

18.1.95

Contents

The Editors and Contributors

JOHN BOWEN was educated at Trinity Hall, Cambridge and the Centre for Contemporary Cultural Studies, Birmingham. He has taught at the City of Birmingham Polytechnic, and is now lecturer in English at Keele University. He has published articles on literary theory, nineteenth- and twentieth-century literature, and the history of English as an academic discipline.

HARRIET DAVIDSON is associate professor of English and Comparative Literature at Rutgers University, where she teaches twentieth-century literature and theory. She is the author of *T.S. Eliot and Hermeneutics: Absence and Interpretation in 'The Waste Land'* (1985), and of articles on contemporary women poets and theory. She is now working on a book on postmodernism and poetry.

TONY DAVIES is senior lecturer in English at the University of Birmingham. He is the author (with Janet Batsleer and others) of *Rewriting English: Cultural Politics of Gender and Class* (1985) and of many articles on renaissance and modern writing and the theory and practice of English teaching. He has edited Milton's *Selected Shorter Poems and Prose* (1989) and *Selected Longer Poems and Prose* (1992), and is currently writing a book about humanism.

STEVE ELLIS is senior lecturer in English at the University of

Birmingham, where he teaches mainly in the areas of medieval, romantic and modern poetry. He is the author of *Dante and English Poetry: Shelley to T.S. Eliot* (1983), *The English Eliot: Design, Language and Landscape in 'Four Quartets'* (1991) and of two collections of poetry. His verse translation of Dante's *Inferno* will be published by Chatto & Windus in 1994.

TONY PINKNEY is lecturer in English at Lancaster University. He is the author of *Women in the Poetry of T.S. Eliot: A Psychoanalytic Approach* (1984), *D.H. Lawrence* (1990) and *Raymond Williams: Postmodern Novelist* (1991), and is currently working on a study of the work of Fredric Jameson. He edited Raymond Williams's posthumous collection, *The Politics of Modernism* (1989), and is a member of the Raymond Williams Memorial Trust. He has recently become associate director of the Wordsworth Centre at Lancaster University.

NIGEL WOOD is a lecturer in the School of English at the University of Birmingham. He is the author of a study of Jonathan Swift and of several essays on literary theory. He is also editor of a selection from Fanny Burney's diaries and journals, *John Gay and the Scriblerians* (with Peter Lewis) and three *Theory in Practice* volumes (on *The Prelude*, *Mansfield Park* and *Don Juan*).

Editors' Preface

The object of this series is to help bridge the divide between the understanding of theory and the interpretation of individual texts. Students are therefore introduced to theory in practice. Although contemporary critical theory is now taught in many colleges and universities, it is often separated from the day-to-day consideration of literary texts that is the staple ingredient of most tuition in English. A thorough dialogue between theoretical and literary texts is thus avoided.

Each of these specially commissioned volumes of essays seeks by contrast to involve students of literature in the questions and debates that emerge when a variety of theoretical perspectives are brought to bear on a selection of 'canonical' literary texts. Contributors were not asked to provide a comprehensive survey of the arguments involved in a particular theoretical position, but rather to discuss in detail the implications for interpretation found in particular essays or studies, and then, taking these into account, to offer a reading of the literary text.

This rubric was designed to avoid two major difficulties which commonly arise in the interaction between literary and theoretical texts: the temptation to treat a theory as a bloc of formulaic rules that could be brought to bear on any text with roughly predictable results; and the circular argument that texts are constructed as such merely by the theoretical perspective from which we choose to regard them. The former usually leads to studies that are really just footnotes to the adopted theorists, whereas the latter is effortlessly self-fulfilling.

It would be disingenuous to claim that our interests in the teaching of theory were somehow neutral and not open to debate. The idea for this series arose from the teaching of theory in relation to specific texts. It is inevitable, however, that the practice of theory poses significant questions as to just what 'texts' might be and where the dividing lines between text and context may be drawn. Our hope is that this series will provide a forum for debate on just such issues as these which are continually posed when students of literature try to engage with theory in practice.

Tony Davies
Barbara Rasmussen
Nigel Wood

How to Use this Book

Each of these essays is composed of a theoretical and a practical element. Contributors were asked to identify the main features of their perspective on the text (exemplified by a single theoretical essay or book) and then to illustrate their own attempts to put this into practice.

We realize that many readers new to recent theory will find its specific vocabulary and leading concepts strange and difficult to relate to current critical traditions in most English courses.

The format of this book has been designed to help if this is your situation, and we would advise the following:

(i) Before reading the essays, glance at the editor's introduction where the literary text's critical history is discussed, and

(ii) also at the prefatory information immediately before the essays, where the editor attempts to supply a context for the adopted theoretical position.

(iii) If you would like to develop your reading in any of these areas, turn to the annotated further reading section at the end of the volume, where you will find brief descriptions of those texts that each contributor has considered of more advanced interest. There are also full citations of the texts to which the contributors have referred in the references. It is also possible that more local information will be contained in notes to the essays.

(iv) The contributors have often regarded the chosen theoretical texts as points of departure and it is also in the nature of theoretical discussion to apply and test ideas on a variety of texts. Turn, therefore, to question and answer sections that follow each essay which are designed to allow contributors to comment and expand on their views in more general terms.

A Note on
the Text

All references to Eliot's published poems and plays are to the *Complete Poems and Plays* (Faber, 1969), abbreviated to *CPP*. References to *The Waste Land* (*WL*) are to this edition, with line numbers. Other poems are referenced to *CPP* with page numbers. Abbreviated reference is also made to the following (full publication details supplied in the references):

OPP   *On Poetry and Poets* (Faber, 1957)
SE   *Selected Essays* (Faber, 1951)
SP   *Selected Prose of T.S. Eliot* (Faber, 1975)
SW   *The Sacred Wood: Essays on Poetry and Criticism* (Methuen, 1920)
UPUC *The Use of Poetry and the Use of Criticism* (Faber, 1933)
WLF   *The Waste Land: A Facsimile and Transcript of the Original Drafts* (Faber, 1971)

Grateful acknowledgement is made to Faber and Faber Ltd for permission to quote from *Complete Poems and Plays* and from the above works by T.S. Eliot.

Introduction

NIGEL WOOD

Eliot's career is no loose bundle of unrelated activities but possesses an essential unity . . . Few literary men in our history have so consistently related all their activities to a coherent set of principles . . . In a time of disorder, Eliot moved toward a restoration of order – toward the restoration of order that poetry alone, perhaps, can give.
(Cleanth Brooks, 'T.S. Eliot: Thinker and Artist',
in Tate 1967: 315)

I sat upon the shore
Fishing, with the arid plain behind me
Shall I at least set my lands in order?

(WL, ll. 423–5)

When a poet's mind is perfectly equipped for its work, it is constantly amalgamating disparate experience; the ordinary man's experience is chaotic, irregular, fragmentary.
('The Metaphysical Poets' [1921], SP, 64)

These fragments I have shored against my ruins

(WL, l. 430)

But how can one shore fragments to restore the ruined or at least maintain it for a while longer? What is no longer perceived as unitary can only be passed off as coherent and enduring by wishing away the deeper revelation that all is indeed beyond repair, that the plain is arid, and so the solitary passivity of contemplation is the only consolation. The damage would seem already to have been done. Restoration would have to be the creation of something new, an adequate substitute perhaps, but still an atonement rather than a reconstruction. Is there a sense to be derived from *The Waste Land* that the poetic powers *remedy* matters or just provide the plausive illusion that there are compensations for an arid reality?

For both Eliot (in his opinion on the Metaphysical poets) and Brooks the answer lies specifically in poetry.[1] The Real could not supply meaning, just the experience of dislocation; poetry remedied this by discovering an apprehension of life that both accepted the tension of contrary impulses in a wider framework and yet was at the same time intensely personal:

> We can only say that it appears likely that poets in our civiliza-tion, as it exists at present, must be *difficult*. Our civilization com-prehends great variety and complexity, and this variety and complexity, playing upon a refined sensibility, must produce various and complex results. The poet must become more and more comprehensive, more allusive, more indirect, in order to force if necessary, language into his meaning.
>
> ('The Metaphysical Poets', *SP*, 65)

As reality was, so must poetry become if *individual* meaning was to be retained. Mere imitation of the experience of life would not, in the last analysis, suffice, and yet it should be noted that 'Life' does have its influence on the expression of meaning (if not the meaning itself). Given Eliot's perception of the intractable modernity of 1921, comprehen-siveness is a necessity and involves the deployment of allusion and other modes of indirection. Language cannot speak directly of what it feels as the moment of true expression involves carefully calculated violence done to common discourse, a negotiation that inevitably takes a fragmentary form. The anarchy of unassimilable details, the hallmark of *The Waste Land*, may thus be regarded as the vehicle of Eliot's precise meaning, the poem's array of signifiers not to be confused with its implied global meaning.

In full, the closing passage of the poem runs as follows:

> I sat upon the shore
> Fishing, with the arid plain behind me
> Shall I at least set my lands in order?
> London Bridge is falling down falling down falling down
> *Poi s'ascose nel foco che gli affina*
> *Quando fiam uti chelidon* – O swallow swallow
> *Le Prince d'Aquitaine à la tour abolie*
> These fragments I have shored against my ruins
> Why then Ile fit you. Hieronimo's mad againe.
> Datta. Dayadhvam. Damyata.
> Shantih shantih shantih
>
> (*WL*, ll. 423–33)

At the very least this proclaims the clash of discourses – from innocent playground rhymes to an invocation of the Fisher King myth from Jessie Weston's *From Ritual to Romance* (1920) and her *The Quest of the Holy Grail* (1913) to a fragment from Thomas Kyd's *The Spanish Tragedy* (1584-7?). There is no generic continuity, yet this may simply be a case of a superficial disorder which obliges the reader to search for an underlying 'essential' principle – exactly what some would claim to be the point of the whole poem. If this is accepted, what appears to be a serendipitous collection of allusions is aptly chosen and calculated to provoke an instinctive desire for coherence in the reader.

It is at the close of the poem, too, that we might recognize its mythical elements. Eliot's own Headnote is a playful one, but it does send the interested reader to Weston's work for the thinking behind the title, the plan and 'a good deal of the incidental symbolism'. In the Grail legend the Fisher King presides over lands that have become waste and sterile, a mirror of his own impotence either through sexual mutilation or severe illness. This malaise cannot be cured unless some Quester meet with success in travelling to the Grail chapel, there to undergo several trials, the reward being the ability to recognize the Grail's significance and to interpret the symbols associated with it correctly. Without this, the Waste Land cannot be redeemed. If Eliot took this scheme over into his poem directly, then it does not automatically mean that the closing passage moves towards fulfilment. Weston is analysing a recurrent narrative pattern which springs from a deep human desire to expiate through trial and privation; she is not providing the world with a redemptive story, as she is merely describing a basic need.[2]

Eliot's own note to the repeated closing word points to its position as the formal ending to 'an Upanishad' (the poetic commentary that follows the *Vedas*, the sacred Hindu scriptures), and immediately gives it a Christian resonance: ' "The Peace which passeth understanding" is our equivalent to this word'.[3] This use of Sanskrit resists the immediate decoding of the word into a familiar semantic pattern and exemplifies the quiet that might arrive when the intolerable wrestle with words finishes and we give ourselves up to the peace of acceptance and transcendence. Thus, the penultimate line's trio of Upanishad commands ('give', 'sympathize' and 'control' – the thunder message) advise the penitent to relinquish egoistic demands on the self and to concentrate on the self-discipline that helps one escape the snares of sensual gratification. The poem concludes with a mini-sermon and a benediction.

The overall narrative shape can thus be arranged with this goal in mind. Burying a dead 'heap of broken images' (l. 22) is a prelude to the cruel awakening of memory and desire that the Unreal City forbids. The purgation of the self signalled as necessary by the Fire Sermon is a withdrawal from worldly hopelessness and luxurious opportunism. While empirical reality cannot be absorbed into the wider pattern the heart can still beat 'obedient/To controlling hands' (ll. 421–2).[4] The Waste Land may not be rejuvenated but some of its inhabitants can redeem themselves.

I will return to this passage later, but two matters need to be raised at this juncture: first, the portrayal and exploration of disconnection and the pain of alienation is more extensive and creative than that of the eventual salvation; and second, to regard the closing passage as redemptive might be an example of special pleading. Here there is no hint of those poised lines on unified poetic discourse that appear in 'Little Gidding' from *The Four Quartets* (1943):

> . . . (where every word is at home,
> Taking its place to support the others,
> The word neither diffident nor ostentatious,
> An easy commerce of the old and the new,
> The common word exact without vulgarity . . .)

> > (*CPP*, 197)

Salvation is not manifested in *The Waste Land* by overt rhetorical means; it has to be supplied by and in the reader's careful noting of various allusive contexts and from her/his judgement of what common factors they contain. The reliance on a common reader to accomplish this is remarkable in itself.

The apology for poetry that Eliot advances in his prose from 1919 to 1922 is significant on two counts. First, the division between poetic and other modes of conception (echoed here by Brooks – a representative voice) stresses an aesthetic order that is almost by definition the polar opposite of the more superficial patterns provided by humdrum reality, the dull urban round that produces the genus, Sweeney. In his 'Whispers of Immortality' (which first appeared in the *Little Review* [Chicago] in September 1918) the opening four stanzas appear rather as a versified critique of Jacobean writers, Webster and Donne in particular. The former is praised for seeing the 'skull beneath the skin', (l. 2), whereas the latter.

> found no substitute for sense
> To seize and clutch and penetrate;
> Expert beyond experience . . .
>
> *(CPP, 52)*

Here the apparent oxymoron of a 'sense' that reaches beyond 'experience' is glossed by references to 'the anguish of the marrow' (l. 13) and the uncontrollable 'fever of the bone' (l. 16) that are *too* corporeal for quotidian experience. It is enough to stand distinct from the second movement of the poem, the depiction of the rank feline attractions and luxuries of Grishkin's drawing-room existence that admit no 'metaphysics' or even any thought at all. Instead of revulsion at the charnel-house skulls uncovered by the searching eyes of both writers there is a sardonic power in the determination to find some bedrock of common fate to highlight, and so dilute the fascination with, 'lusts and luxuries' (l. 8) that actually seems the key to modern perception.[5] Eliot is never happier or more assured that he has encountered the Real than when his spade has hit bone.

There is here a nostalgia for a past social formation that was able to confront mortality without flinching. In his 1921 essay, it was this quality of Donne's that was the most impressive: the instant coincidence of thought and feeling, so that one could 'feel [a] thought as immediately as the odour of a rose'. Thoughts for Donne were an 'experience' in that they 'modified his sensibility' (*SP*, 64). We, however, inherit a culture where this is an impossible ideal for even the most poetic of souls; sensibility is dissociated from thought and the truths of poetry from those of philosophy, on the one hand, and from the generalized proverbs that actually determine modern behaviour, on the other.

Second, there is the belief that Eliot's readers could, by means of indirection, find direction out. So blatantly allusive is *The Waste Land* that the search for some core meaning has to take in a myriad of brief literary references which in their turn invite the fatal victory of the academic footnote, or at least Eliot's own serio-comic commentary. It is the strategy of the poem that it *appears* not to be fully resonant until we assess how the various allusive contexts we trace square with our notion of the poetic totality, the sum of its individual tropes. Although composed of hand-me-down material, this achieved fabric must be new. This might not only be true of *The Waste Land*, but also of all poetry: 'a degree of heterogeneity of material compelled into unity by the operation of the poet's mind is omnipresent in poetry' ('The Metaphysical Poets', *SP*, 61). Note the need to exhibit compulsion and effort, the victory of art over its recalcitrant material. If we were to trace the divining hand of the poet over the whole work too easily, then the writing could testify equally easily to the authority of the artist and a victory at little cost. There is a risk here which the critical history of the poem manifests as central to many readings of the work. What if the poetic experience of order were denied or the poem failed to imply a new 'metaphysical' cohesion? Instead of affirmation, what if the resort to the closing mantra illustrated a glorious failure of hope? What if we find Eliot's analysis of Modernity unconvincing?

A 'Literature out of Literature'

The Waste Land first appeared, in the first issue of Eliot's own magazine, *Criterion*, in Great Britain in October 1922, and in *The Dial* in the USA a month later. Although it is probable that the accompanying 'Notes on the Waste Land' had been completed as early as July of that year, neither issue of these influential literary reviews carried them alongside the poetry. According to Valerie Eliot in the Introduction to her edition of the poem's original drafts, a contractual agreement had been struck on this in September between Gilbert Seldes (managing director of *The Dial*) and the eventual publishers of the poem in book form, Boni and Liveright. Prior publication was to be allowed Seldes, but the fuller version was first to appear in the USA with Liveright's imprint, the Notes necessary, not to ensure comprehension of the poem, but rather to swell the contents to book length.[6] Accordingly, the Notes were first available in the USA in December, and then with Leonard Woolf's Hogarth Press in September 1923 (each book hand-printed). The role of the Notes is examined in this volume on pages

103–4. There is no indication that Eliot ever felt the loss of his own annotation a serious matter for the well-read readership of both reviews. *The Dial* was an established arbiter of avant-garde taste and from 1920 had employed Ezra Pound as its Paris correspondent, whereas Eliot was floating the *Criterion* with his poem and was soon to include Pound, the short stories of Virginia Woolf, an autobiographical fragment of Yeats and criticism by Eliot, Herbert Read and Marcel Proust. Conceivably, the annotation contained *some* nuggets of authorial intention amidst the cod pedantries, and fitted the poem not only for individual publication but to ensure that the otherwise subtextual directions of the work were more accessible – but to whom? While their exposition is generally helpful to the specialist, it can hardly have been designed to elucidate the recondite material that a casual reader would find basic to initial intelligibility.[7]

In 1956 Eliot could afford to look back on the critical apparatus with regret, for he had at first intended merely to 'put down all the references for [his] quotations' as a defensive gesture, 'spiking the guns of critics of [his] earlier poems who had accused [him] of plagiarism' and yet to do this with a coat-trailing 'bogus scholarship' ('The Frontiers of Criticism', *OPP*, 109). The Notes were to gesture (perhaps impatiently) to the implicit pattern that would also ensure that his originality in synthesizing his allusions did not go unnoticed. This doubtful retrospection is, however, very much part of the later Eliot. As Grover Smith remarks: 'Self-criticism which would substitute hindsight for past vision is like historical revisionism. In both cases a new *historian* appears, but the things that happened in the past happened nevertheless' (Smith 1983: 49). A parade of ultra-pedantry may indeed accomplish something very precise, and it is clear from the earliest reviews of the book-length version that much was achieved by the Notes. The Cambridge scholar, F.L. Lucas, in the *New Statesman* (3 November 1923) distrusted the poem's obscure 'Alexandrianism', which replaced 'depth by muddiness, beauty by echoes, passion by necrophily' and which was fostered by the annotation: ' . . . a poem that has to be explained in notes is not unlike a picture with "This is a dog" inscribed beneath' (Grant 1982, I: 195, 199). Charles Powell in the *Manchester Guardian* (31 October 1923) was more swingeing and at the same time more pertinent. Foxed by the discontinuities in tone and narrative, he found it a 'mad medley' that would elude the 'ordinary reader'. He had to conclude that it had a plan,

> because its author says so; and presumably it has some meaning, > because he speaks of its symbolism; but meaning, plan, and

intention alike are massed behind a smoke-screen of anthropological and literary erudition, and only the pundit, the pedant, or
the clairvoyant will be in the least aware of them.

(Grant 1982, I: 194)

There is nothing perennially populist about poetry, and I have already
quoted Eliot's observation that modern verse *had* to be complex to cap-
ture a post-Edwardian age,[8] but the Notes advertise this eccentricity,
and evidently did not elucidate sufficiently. It is a possibility that that
was not their design. The effect of modernism on art in general will be
reviewed below, but it might here be relevant to mention just one
literary characteristic of such a tendency, namely, that the hitherto well-
crafted poem, autonomous and lyrical, was exposed as a cosmetic exercise (see p. 23). A consciousness of modernity demanded a searching
interrogation of the traditions that had scripted 'normal' readerly
involvement in literature and definitions of its scope. It should come as
no surprise, then, that the modernist in Eliot should set out to confound
the reader by whatever textual resources were open to him. (That the
term 'modernist' is not quite adequate in describing the Eliot of early
career, I would readily agree – see pp. 18–24.) This anxiety about a
secure authorial intention can be traced in several (mainly British)
reviews. Several readers assumed that *The Waste Land* was a loose title
for several autonomous poems and others that it represented a rather
heavy-handed joke.[9]

In the USA, on the other hand, it was not only Eliot's Notes which
'helped' the reader; Seldes, director of *The Dial*, was determined to give
Eliot a ready-made achievement. At the contractual meeting in
September, it had also been agreed that *The Waste Land* was to receive
The Dial's annual award for poetry worth $2,000. It also came with a
commissioned review in the December issue by Edmund Wilson
entitled 'The Poetry of Drouth' (revised for his *Axel's Castle* (1931)).
The central perception that focuses Wilson's reading is that the whole
poem forms a 'concrete image of a spiritual drouth' and that it is
organized in terms of *poetic* effect, for, given its evident roots in a 'con-
stricted emotional experience' and its 'lack of structural unity', the work
is affecting and stems from one who can feel 'intensely and with distinction and [with Wilson's eye surely not securely on the object] speaks
naturally in beautiful verse' (Grant 1982, I: 140, 143). For all his determination to find the poem distinctive, Wilson, when pressed for an
account of the work's unity, falls back on lyrical criteria: that it is the
anguished cry of a soul in distress, modulating into the accents of

Tiresias, Buddha and the Sibyl, but retaining a consistent *poetic* texture. As we shall see (pp. 25-6), the very definition of the 'poetic' at this time was the subject of staunchly conducted debate, so where Wilson feels at a loss to come to terms with the exact contours of Eliot's writing, it now seems a pragmatic manoeuvre for him to claim it for the mysteries of poetry.

This was no isolated example, however, and the early supportive reviews for the poem stemmed, directly or indirectly, from *The Dial* or *Criterion* axis, wedded to an as yet unformulaic modernism. Seldes himself approached the work via the criticism in his piece for the New York *Nation* (6 December 1922) and, in terms that were to predict much later preoccupations, showed an appreciation of 'ideas' in poetry and the 'aesthetic problem' any new work will present. To be a critic is to be the self-conscious reader, who hunts a 'statement of the structures in which our perceptions, when we face a work of art, form themselves' (Grant 1982, I: 146). Unity is not perhaps to be expected of problematic and radical novelty. Similarly, Conrad Aiken, when attempting his 'Anatomy of Melancholy' in the *New Republic* (7 February 1923), found its introverted allusions the product of a theory of society and readerly response:

> Mr. Eliot's sense of the literary past has become so overmastering as almost to constitute the motive of the work. It is as if . . . he wanted to make a 'literature out of literature' – a poetry not more actuated by life itself than by poetry; as if he had concluded that the characteristic awareness of a poet of the 20th century must inevitably, or ideally, be a very complex and very literary awareness able to speak only, or best, in terms of the literary past . . .
> (Grant 1982, I: 157)[10]

Here is a provoking challenge that *The Waste Land* sets before readers who would prefer the poem either to exhibit a unified consciousness or to subordinate (by clear definition) the allusive power to some gradually unfolding mimetic design. Eliot does not even locate a past Golden Age in the epic manners of some Homeric or Virgilian heroes,[11] but rather constructs a kaleidoscope of scattered and broken references that do not indicate some particular historical location for his Utopia – because he denies both that it exists and that it is even workable as an ideal.

Adverse early reviews did not affect sales of the work. Indeed, a second impression followed before 1923 was out. Gradually, though, Eliot's interest in the poem seemed to abate. He had written to Richard Aldington on 15 November 1922, that he regarded it as 'a thing of the past' and that he was 'feeling toward a new form and style' (quoted in Grant 1982, I: 22). This may have been wishful thinking, as he was to assemble his retrospective *Poems 1909–1925* for Faber and Gwyer to appear on 23 November 1925. In purely personal terms, however, Eliot may well have felt that the final appearance of the much-worked *Waste Land* was a necessary rite of passage.

In time the poem gained notoriety as well as a fair measure of fame. It frequently became the object of a debate about whether the extremes of modernism were worth it. John Crowe Ransom, the influential editor of the *Kenyon Review* and one of the earliest moving forces of New Criticism (see note 22, p. 145), actually encountered the work's disconnectedness as if it were the 'apotheosis of modernity', compact with all the 'specifically modern errors . . . as if it were the function of art to break down the usual singleness of the artistic image'. Art retained wholeness and did not embrace chaos: 'For imagination things cohere; pluralism cannot exist when we relax our obsessions and allow such testimony as is in us to come out' ('Waste Lands', *New York Evening Post Literary Review* [14 July 1923], Grant 1982, I: 176–7). Allen Tate's trenchant rejoinder in the 4 August issue of the *Post* took the form of a letter of protest, preferring the open system of Eliot's aesthetic and its consistent irony to Ransom's formalism (see Grant 1982, I: 180–2).

The impression is of battle lines drawn up on the poem that is used as a convenient pretext to debate larger issues. On the one side there is a Romantic unity of discourse, and on the other there is the at times harsh 'music of ideas', where 'its symbols are not mystical but emotional', to borrow I.A. Richards's phrasing from the appendix to the revised edition of his extremely influential *Principles of Literary Criticism* (1924; 1926) (Grant 1982, I: 236–7). There was available, however, another emphasis among those who might have shared the same ground rules of appreciation. For F.R. Leavis, the structure is more a mythical one than an expression of personal despair. Noting Richards's musical analogy, he is drawn to the poem's tone and Eliot's careful management of it, but he is more at pains than predecessors to stress that this is a 'self-subsistent poem' (Leavis 1932: 94) that can function poetically without the author's annotational help. Its elitism is due to the age that provided the work's readership, an overly complex urban jungle: the 'Machine Age' where 'breach of continuity and the uprooting of life' spell the end of a 'life rooted in the soil' (Leavis 1932: 78). This is not an opinion that seems to vary much from Richards's or even Tate's verdict on the poem in that it honours its 'inclusive human consciousness' (Leavis 1932: 81), but Leavis's pastoral perspective actually emphasized its more mimetic qualities. Its despair was that of a generation, and the only mode of such expression was an inevitably attenuated one.

It is significant that Eliot noted this central distinction between the mythical and the narrative kinds of poetic organization early during the immediate reception of the poem. In his 'Ulysses, Order, and Myth' (Dial, November 1923), his defence of the risks Joyce took with his multifarious and polyphonic narrative are noted and applauded:

> In using a myth, in manipulating a continuous parallel between contemporaneity and antiquity, Mr. Joyce is pursuing a method which others must pursue after him . . . It is simply a way of controlling, of ordering, of giving a shape and a significance to the immense panorama of futility and anarchy which is contemporary history.
>
> (SP, 177)

Joyce had published the earlier chapters of Ulysses in the Egoist in 1919 and was working on the later ones during the first months of 1921. As both works appeared in 1922 there is a critical tendency to trace just resemblances between the two and so approach them both as primarily modernist texts. As Helen Gardner pointed out in 1949, the two texts differ significantly. Whereas Eliot's work is imbued with a pervasive sense of sin, Joyce celebrates an escape from personal responsibility: 'His imagination is not haunted by either the presence or the absence of God' (Gardner 1949: 86). More pertinent to the debate on the poem's type of unity, however, is Gardner's concise account of their respective use of mythic material. Joyce achieves 'coherence by means of plot' by providing extensive allusive parallels to Homer's Odyssey, 'one of the most shapely and beautifully designed poems', where Eliot 'discards plot and his poem has no conclusion or solution'. What coherence it has derives from its musical qualities ('repetition and variation') and the glances towards the Fisher King myth – which do not signal closure at all, but merely a central predicament, 'omitting any of the solutions of the predicament which we find in the various Grail stories'. We may gradually trace the progress of Ulysses towards Bloom's final homecoming and the final setting of lands in order, but The Waste Land, 'if it moves at all', cannot muster this sense of finality as it gestures 'towards some moment which is outside the poem and may never come' (Gardner 1949: 86–7).[12] This separation of narrative from formal enjoyment is a perennial concern of the criticism of the mid-1950s onwards, and anticipates the more recent theoretical concern with aspects of Eliot's poetic *ethos* and its anticipated readerly response.

Whereas narrative unity implies linear development and a storyteller, where apparently disconnected items or events are eventually discovered to have a function as part of a global symbol, Eliot's enactment of futility and the anarchic threat to accepted cultural values is a difficult critical problem. Where can the author be traced? If the writer's design is not part of the dramatic play of conflicts directly inferred from the text (that is, one that cannot be illustrated by direct quotation), how can one approach the work except by the imaginative involvement of an inspired guess? For Gardner, the key is Christianity and Eliot's realization that a full awakening to devotional realities involves a necessary descent into Hell before the hope of purgation, but for most readers in the 1950s and 1960s, doubtless influenced by New Criticism, the poetry lay in the work's complex tensions and irony, textual pleasures not mimetic ones.[13] If the author's design involved an absence of direct address, then the role of the reader is redesigned to cope with this. It was not until this gathering appreciation of the implied reader became obvious and part of the critical 'common sense' applied not just to *The Waste Land* but to all writing that Eliot's own terms for interpretation were challenged. It should be no surprise that his standing as a modernist was also questioned.

Pound and the Heap of Broken Images

With the appearance of the poem's manuscript and draft facsimiles in 1971 and Lyndall Gordon's *Early Years* biography in 1977 we have only recently been in a position to assess quite how much the heap of broken images reflected (the historical) Eliot's own state of mind and the actual existence of the poetic materials before Ezra Pound intervened and helped edit them. Pound was thanked for his work on the manuscripts and typescript with the dedication to him as '*il miglior fabbro*' ('the better craftsman') when the poem was included in Eliot's *Poems 1909–1925* (1925). It might have been addressed to him as the better editor, however, as the final form of the work is directly indebted to his intercession when he set to work on Eliot's varied and unconnected verses in Paris in January 1922.

The *Waste Land Facsimile* (Eliot 1971) establishes the extent of Pound's involvement and also how very much the finished poem resembled his own distinct artistic tastes. Eliot alone could not have written the poem as we now have it. This was due to two significant crises of which he was acutely conscious, one personal and the other to do with his own relationship with an audience for his poems. Both Eliot and his wife were in fragile health. Vivien had had a breakdown in March–April 1921, and Eliot, with his 'long poem' and the launch of *The Criterion* seriously stalled, began to suffer, too. From 12 October, in a highly nervous and emotionally disordered state, he was granted three months' leave from the bank which he spent first with Vivien in Margate and then from November alone in Lausanne. While he took the very first drafts of several sections with him, it is likely that this was the most intensive period of composition ('In the mountains, there you feel free' (*WL*, l. 17)). Writing a poem on spiritual drought and a hope (no more?) of redemption is clearly suitable for a writer in this frame of mind, so it is no surprise to find those warming to a confessional theme citing this autobiographical evidence.

There was also a less localized problem that troubled Eliot throughout the long period of shoring his fragments for his long poem. How could he keep faith in a long-term narrative strategy when most of his earlier work had stressed the isolated image or symbol and left the reader to register its implicit impact? In 'The Love Song of J. Alfred Prufrock' and also 'Portrait of a Lady' (1915; published in 1917) Eliot split the reader's attention between a tentative first-person narrator and an antagonistic, or at best diffident, social milieu. Both poems dramatize the impossibility of true interpersonal communication:

> And I must borrow every changing shape
> To find expression . . . dance, dance
> Like a dancing bear . . .
>
> (*CPP*, 21)

Where such personae were not expressly called for, where Eliot evoked mood by extended symbol or image (his symbolist/imagist work), this problematic portrayal of 'personality' only seemed to be shelved. In 'Preludes' (1910–11; published in 1917), for example, he commenced the poem by attempting an unsparing mood picture of dingy urban life, a string of 'objective correlatives' where an exact emotional state found meaning in an apparently blank cityscape. In the midst of this mechanical outer life Eliot does resort to an expression of personality near the poem's close:

> I am moved by fancies that are curled
> Around these images, and cling:
> The notion of some infinitely gentle
> Infinitely suffering thing.
>
> (*CPP*, 23)

When we are returned to the impersonality of the last lines, it is now motivated by this compassion. We are directed by the human factor to take the otherwise neutral observation as an index of feeling. The first person is a direct function of the whole, not an axis of interest in itself. As Grover Smith notes, the procedure was not an expansive one and the later satires only accentuated this tendency: the move to caricature was not 'intended to be satiric, but clinical . . . Eliot's personages . . . were designed to miss the condition of satire, because they crystallise human nature instead of exaggerating it . . . They were *mythic*' (Smith 1983: 9). The difficulty lay in embracing the 'mythic' (some over-arching, if implicit, framework) while *extending*, not contracting, its operations. The result was the heap of images or single poems passed to Pound which were too broken in their cumulative effect to add up to the 'long poem' or universal statement towards which Eliot wanted to progress.

The most radical changes carried out on Pound's advice or simply as a result of Eliot's second thoughts were mainly in the direction of a more compact and so less immediately accessible poem. Tony Sharpe's review of the changes is accurate:

> The original was a curious intermingling of the spontaneously right and the laboriously wrong . . . By removing the overt denunciations and by breaking up the regular verses, whose orderliness laid claim to an unearned authority, Pound diminished the element of assertiveness and encouraged a poem which was less a statement than it was an enactment, and more a confession than an indictment.
>
> (Sharpe 1991: 90–1)[14]

For example, 'The Fire Sermon' was originally different in both length and style. Opening with some seventy lines of rhyming couplets (a parody of Pope's mock-heroic idiom in his *Rape of the Lock*), depicting an empty-headed lady of fashion called Fresca, the section was overtly satirical and contained a hard edge of sexual distaste. Fresca could be 'autumn's favourite in a furnished flat,/Or strolling slattern in a tawdry gown,/A doorstep dunged by every dog in town' (ll. 49–51; *WLF*, 27). Pound cut this section entirely, as also a later passage of fifteen lines, where Londoners became 'phantasmal gnomes' (l. 113; *WLF*, 31). Pound's marginal notes run 'B-ll-s' and 'Palmer Cox's brownies' – a reference to the popular American illustrator of a series of children's books starring a group of well-disposed elves. To Pound, Eliot's attempt at an insidiously decorous style of denunciation seemed insufferably coy, and, worse, it left the casual coupling of typist and clerk that followed rather more polemical and directly critical of just city culture.

The largest excision occurred in the 'Death by Water' section, which originally detailed a long account (over ninety-two lines) of a disastrous sea voyage where the fateful end is accompanied by necessary intoxication ('. . . Home and mother./Wheres a cocktail shaker, Ben, heres plenty of cracked ice' (79–80; *WLF*, 69)). There are several changes marked by Pound, although the decision to jettison the whole was Eliot's. His instincts were towards five sections containing lines more equally distributed, yet this should not mean that he always conceived the work as unified. The idea that it was a loose collection of associated yet separate poems was entertained until late in the revision process. Pound looked back from January 1931 and considered Eliot's original suggestion to publish it in instalments an 'outrage', claiming that he had had to howl 'to high heaven' to get it printed 'whole' (Pound 1951: 310). He was, however, to describe it as 'a very important sequence of poems' in the *New Age* as late as 30 March (see Stock 1970: 309). Eliot, too, could consider his first thoughts as too prolix. April was the cruellest month, in 'The Burial of the Dead', only after the depiction of a boys' night out, apparently in Boston. The typescript shows Eliot's own suggested deletion on what was presumably the copy that Pound received.

The title Eliot first gave the poem was 'He Do The Police In Different Voices'. There is already the hint here of a deliberately recondite proceeding, as the reference is to a well-hidden episode in Charles Dickens's *Our Mutual Friend* (1864–5), where Sloppy, a foundling taken in by an old widow, Betty Higden, is praised for his reading aloud of newspapers: 'You mightn't think it, but Sloppy is a beautiful reader of a newspaper. He do the Police in different voices' (ch. xvi; Dickens 1971: 246). This is apposite for a number of reasons. First, Dickens's narrative experiments in the book are marked. Changes of perspective, the apparently disconnected plots and multiple centres of interest are part of the freight Eliot took over from Dickens. Second, the setting for the tales is a debased and (in Eliot's terms) unreal London, full of predominantly superficial human types, often driven by base greed. Third, the novel, which is predominantly a social satire, often resorts to the narrative *topos* of drowning (or supposed death by water). John Harmon is attacked and left unconscious by thieves on his return to England. He narrowly escapes drowning in the Thames, while a man of similar build is mistaken for him. Harmon seizes his chance to learn more about the fate of his inheritance during his exile abroad by taking an assumed name. 'Gaffer' Hexam, a boatman who also plies a salvage trade and who picked up the corpse, is accidentally drowned. Headstone and Riderhood are both drowned after their tussle by a river lock, yet Wrayburn (a hero) is rescued from drowning, when near to death, by Lizzie Hexam. It would be overinterpretation to claim that the Thames or water fulfils some basic thematic function in the novel, but it flows as a metonymic reminder of the depredations of the city and also of rebirth and possible new opportunity (witness the 'resurrections' of Harmon and Wrayburn). In Jessie Weston's account of Nature and Rebirth rituals, it should be remembered, drowning was often a prelude to unlikely resuscitation (see Weston 1980: 51–2).

These are narrative similarities, but there is a more pervasive concern that is highlighted the more we examine the extremely cryptic reference contained in this first title. How many readers could be expected to trace the above relation between Dickens and the poem? If Eliot had intended some more publicly available reference, we must presume that he could have found one. Sloppy is such a minor character, Betty Higden's verdict on his histrionic ability so incidental, that the choice at first seems perverse and even pedantic. The fact that we have to pursue research to perceive the link is a further potentially revealing association that could have been crucial about this first draft and Eliot's dimly perceived first intentions: a sense of connection is not obvious in the modern city, as a tangential or even hermetic detail may be the key to an otherwise hidden truth.[15] Indeed, it is the very condition of Eliot's truth that it *is* hidden and remote from common experience. Sloppy is elevated by this seemingly random choice into a type of mindless urban ventriloquist. When not hard at the mechanical and menial work of turning a mangle handle, his one distinctive claim to fame is to provide a special voice, borrowing the intentions of others, to spread the uncreating word with the addition of a little specious showmanship. This is one of the signs of the fatal divorce between feeling and intellect that Eliot observed was characteristic of the modern human condition.

More details that might help us recognize the earliest preoccupations of this first *Waste Land* are slight alterations of emphasis between draft and printed copy in the closing lines that I started by examining (pp. 2–4). I approached them there as if there were a concealed continuity in the lines leading to a final embrace of metaphysical peace. This involves reading between the lines and linking what at face value may be a chance arrangement of fragments. The process of reading, the need to find some intelligible frame for the lines, is thus a *necessary* ingredient of their full meaning, indeed helps enact such a meaning. One could go further and claim that the success at tracing a covert sense helps enlist support for the proposition that a global meaning (God?) exists. As originally composed, these lines included the quotation from *The Spanish Tragedy* ('Why then Ile fit you') with the play's subtitle ('Hieronimo's mad againe') as the sixth from last. Eliot's manuscript shows that positioning cancelled and the final printed order instated – third from the end – perhaps to introduce its threat of furious insanity nearer the poised final coda to the poem. There is another subtle afterthought in this passage and this concerns the last line, not in content, but in typographical arrangement. 'Shantih shantih shantih' follows without a gap as the poem was printed, but, as per the typescript left with Pound, a deliberate gap of two lines preceded it – perhaps to suggest that this peace does not lead on from the preceding passage, but rather has to be embraced in isolation from it, as a desperate measure. These may be slight alterations, but crucial ones.

The madness of Hieronimo is due to his intense thirst for revenge after the murder of his son, Horatio. The actual murderers (Lorenzo and Balthazar) cannot be brought to justice by official means, so Hieronimo resorts to a desperate ruse: to persuade them to perform parts in a play to be performed before the court, during which they are actually killed. This madness is part of the intense desire for justice and not what we may call a clinical condition. It is associated with a secret mission that would not be countenanced if widely known (Eliot's satiric purpose?):

> Why then I'll fit you; say no more.
> When I was young I gave my mind
> And plied myself to fruitless poetry:
> Which though it profit the professor naught,
> Yet is it passing pleasing to the world.
>
> (Kyd 1985: IV.i.70–4)

The world's pleasure cannot be shared by the poet. Yet there is a further relevance to the involvement of the play. When handing out the parts for this play-within-a-play, Hieronimo designs it as a spectacle with varied accents and idioms: 'Each one of us must act his part/In unknown languages'. The result of this is the 'fall of Babylon [an earlier unreal metropolis],/Wrought by the heavens in this confusion' (Kyd 1985: IV.i.172–3, 195–6).[16]

There is no clear agenda to emerge from this source-finding and it is pursued with the important reservation in mind that, just because we can now bring this material to bear on the overt text, that does not guarantee its validity as a guide to Eliot's conscious intention. What is obvious from this is that the work of interpretation cannot proceed with any certainty that a limit is *intended*. Allusions can provoke a relay of associations. Eliot confessed in his note to line 46 in 'The Burial of the Dead' that he was 'not familar with the exact constitution of the Tarot pack of cards, from which [he had] obviously departed to suit [his] own convenience'.[17] There is no legislating for private associations.

In this, Eliot is enough of a Modernist to merit the name, but there are areas of *The Waste Land* that, if not actually resistant to this label, should remind us that all Modernist documents can be so in their own way.

Tradition and Modernism

When introducing Pound's literary essays in 1954, Eliot stressed that this was not only advice from a practitioner and teacher, but also from one whose motive was 'the refreshment, revitalisation, and "making new" of literature in our own time' (Pound 1954: xiii). This is not just a commitment to the evolution of what is perceived as an inherited tradition but rather a revolution of ideas where the relevance of a shared tradition or culture is questioned root and branch. To identify and value modernity is also to locate a guiding and significant difference between one's cultural inheritance and the demands of the new moment. This affects both the preparation of the artist and how she/he might communicate with the intended readership or audience. Modernism is distinctive in its putting into crisis the accepted norms of this relationship and in its challenge to the bases on which art might be both comprehensible and affecting. A gap between the artist and audience is both established and exploited. The avant-garde is not just elitist in practice, an approach to art that is perhaps deduced by astute criticism, but also part of a programme to redefine how art forms part of society. Eliot is not alone in concluding that *new* art must be complex and that the emotions of the poet must be distinct not only from those of the intended readers but even from those experienced by the artist's 'normal' historical self.

One abiding problem in judging Eliot's view of Modernist art in early career is that he did not know that he was producing it. The term is a retrospective deduction, and probably only became critical currency in 1927 with Robert Graves and Laura Riding's *A Survey of Modernist*

Poetry. Here the term signifies any work that provides such a level of specialized expression that it first presents itself as challenging in its obscurity. Readers have, therefore, to be conscious of their efforts to 'make sense' of it. It does not make concessions to the reader because it forms an attempt to be distant from 'normal' expectations, attaining an almost impersonal status as an art form in and for itself. It therefore does not serve some pre-existing dogma or thesis, as its special and irreducible nature is supposed to be, and not mean. The criticism most associated with this aspiration is New Criticism, with its definition both of considerations of the author or original context of composition and also the recording of considerations of artistic effect as 'intentional' and 'affective' fallacies, respectively.

When Eliot identified Joyce's 'mythical method' in 1923, he did not regard it merely as a well-chosen option out of several others available, but the only one that could make 'the modern world possible for art, towards . . . order and form' (*SP*, 178). In this, Eliot thought of himself as a latter-day 'classicist', stressing how the basic myths that are normally disguised from our consciousness in daily existence should claim our attention. As Lyndall Gordon has pointed out, however, he often thought of himself as at best a fellow-traveller with Pound and Roger Fry (whom he had first met in 1916) (see Gordon 1977: 66–9). Pound's firm belief in hard-edged images that aimed to produce their own reality was enviably lucid yet possibly unsubtle.

As early as the summer of 1912, Pound claimed that he, 'H.D.' (Hilda Doolittle) and Richard Aldington had agreed on three principles:

1 Direct treatment of the 'thing' whether subjective or objective.
2 To use absolutely no word that does not contribute to the presentation.
3 As regarding rhythm: to compose in the sequence of the musical phrase, not in sequence of a metronome.

This resulted in a stylistic interest in the iconic image, the founding characteristic of the 'Imagist' vogue for isolated experiences that are not allowed to be modified or introduced by neighbouring narrative events or sentiments: in this regard, images present 'an intellectual and emotional complex in an instant of time' that is so instantaneous in effect that there is given a 'sense of sudden liberation; that sense of freedom from time limits and space limits' ('A Retrospect' [1918], Pound 1954: 3–4). This distrust of the abstract formulation or preconceived intention did much to harden Eliot's *Waste Land* drafts.[18] For Pound serious art is so 'perfectly controlled' that it is capable of saying just what is meant with no redundant padding, a goal of 'complete clarity and simplicity' ('The Serious Artist' [1913], Pound 1954: 50).

Pound was ready to lionize *The Waste Land* as early as July 1922, dubbing it 'the justification of the "movement", of our modern experiment, since 1900' (Pound 1951: 248). He was duly pleased to help this to come to light, but there is much already of this form of Modernism in the work that Eliot handed over to Pound. C.K. Stead has called this a 'poetics of juxtaposition', where 'self-sufficient yet linked illuminations' are not produced as an artistic unity by a clear narrative or even by a consistent discursive mood (Stead 1986: 87). This is exactly the kind of material on which editorial work can be creative in *constituting* a poetic unity. Eliot's determination to mould a long poem out of such initially unpromising material is part of a project to provide a new model for the long poem that is derived neither from the models of epic nor subjective autobiography, the growth of a poet's mind (for example, Wordsworth's *Prelude*, published in 1850).

This project to write at length is foreign to the rules outlined by Pound and the other first wave of modernists. When he turned to *Hugh Selwyn Mauberley* (1920), the disguised dialogue with Eliot points to a pervasive difference between the two poets. For Pound, Eliot's dilatoriness, his strain of fantasy and confession, was a weak spot.[19] There is no doubting Eliot's appreciation of Modernist art, for his visit to a performance of Stravinsky's *Le Sacre du Printemps* in the summer of 1921 moved him greatly. To a writer struggling with the instinct both to isolate and dissect experience and yet also to provide a motivation or reason behind it, the music suggested an answer in its transformation of 'the rhythm of the steppes into the scream of the motor-horn, the rattle of machinery, the grind of wheels, the beating of iron and steel, the roar of the underground railway, and the other barbaric noises of modern life'. Here was mystery *and* an eerie form of simplicity, and yet the basic myth was too simple, a 'pageant of primitive culture':

> It was interesting to anyone who had read *The Golden Bough*, but hardly more than interesting. In art there should be interpenetration and metamorphosis. Even *The Golden Bough* can be read in two ways: as a collection of entertaining myths, or as a revelation of that vanished mind of which our mind is a continuation.
>
> (Eliot's 'London Letter', October, *The Dial*, 71, July–December, 1921, 452–3)

Here there is no mention of the isolation of the disinterested aesthetic object. Eliot is taken with rhythm and non-mimetic pattern, and not impressed with primitive myth-making.[20]

There is one major reason why the link with Pound's 'Imagist' Modernism seems weak at this point, and that is his distinctive understanding of Tradition. Eliot was no innocent acolyte. His pleasure in Stravinsky's work does not derive from its total novelty, but rather from its submerged continuity with the primitive 'mind'. When assembling Pound's poems for his selection in 1928, Eliot took the opportunity to deny the possibility of true 'invention' (that is, the creation of something out of nothing): 'True originality is merely development; and if it is right development it may appear in the end so *inevitable* that we almost come to the point of view of denying all "original" virtue to the poet' (Pound 1933: x–xi). His 'Reflections on "Vers Libre" ' (*New Statesman*, 3 March 1917) concentrated on dampening revolutionary enthusiasm, when he claimed that 'there is no freedom in art', or rather, 'freedom is only truly freedom when it appears against the background of an artificial limitation' (*SP*, 32, 35). All contemporary perception is thus foreknown.

When Conrad Aiken testified to Eliot's provision of a 'literary' literature, it is likely that he had read what has arguably proved to be Eliot's most famous essay, 'Tradition and the Individual Talent' (1919; for *The Sacred Wood*, 1920). Its usefulness is assured because it can be read as advocating a cosy *rapprochement* between the past and present:

> No poet, no artist of any art, has his complete meaning alone. His significance, his appreciation is the appreciation of his relation to the dead poets and artists. You cannot value him alone; you must set him, for contrast and comparison, among the dead.
>
> (*SP*, 38)

This is Eliot's dig at those at the fag-end of Romantic individualism, but it is not motivated by an antiquarian spirit. He should not be represented as exhorting poets to be learned and deferential, for this relationship is a flexible one, where the past has also to be receptive to the changing needs of the present, in that the 'new work of art', as soon as it is defined as such, implicitly alters the ideal order of the canon (that is actually a projection of usually unacknowledged modern needs):

> for order to persist after the supervention of novelty, the *whole* existing order must be, if ever so slightly, altered; and so the relations, proportions, values of each work of art toward the whole are readjusted; and this is conformity between the old and new.
>
> (*SP*, 38–9)

This, too, is evidence of the 'historical sense'. In practice, this apparently tentative sense of ideal ordering ('if ever so slightly . . . and this is conformity') is very much a commentary on the radical and baffling *Waste Land*. Derived from the more usual unflattering contrast between the debased present and the imaginative evocation of a golden past, mock-heroic writing can question a sentimental regard for that past by implicitly rendering it now as irrelevant and 'literary'.

The 'order' is an 'ideal' one which, if it is no truism, probably points to at least two different suppositions: first, that it is not capable of clear definition and so is a notion of value and less one of validation ('. . . [the new work's] fitting in is a test of its value'); and second, it entails, in effect, the redefinition of literature's confessional power, in that the autonomy of the new artist can only be observed and exploited securely in the midst of tradition (we moderns may appear to know more than dead writers, but then 'they are that which we know') (*SP*, 39–40). Furthermore, the person regarded as a historical item (who perhaps works for Lloyds Bank) is quite distinct from the 'mind which creates'. The emotions suffered from nine to five are not a guide to the '*significant* emotion' which 'has its life in the poem and not in the history of the poet' (*SP*, 41, 44). Eliot thus insulates the poem from the poet; it inhabits a specifically 'literary' realm and expresses 'feelings which are not in actual emotions at all' (*SP*, 43). It follows, therefore, that tracing a writer's intention is a real critical problem. If, by definition, the *poetic* sentiments cannot be adequately understood by the critic, however immersed in European traditions, then descriptions of immediate cultural context or even the factoring in of considerations of the whole *œuvre* are largely beside the point.

With *The Waste Land* in mind, this elusiveness of the authorial *ethos* is significant. Eliot regards writing as an escape from the self and this 'depersonalization', where the 'substantial unity of the soul' is questioned, is also a discounting of history as a route into the work. What takes its place is a 'medium . . . in which impressions and experiences combine in peculiar and unexpected ways' (*SP*, 40, 42). This is very much the preoccupation of Eliot's early criticism. In 'Tradition' he adopts the view that the critic is a self-analyst, committed to 'articulating what passes in our minds when we read a book and feel an emotion about it, for criticizing our own minds in their work of criticism' (*SP*, 37), but this need not be the shadow rather than the substance, for critic readers have to judge an 'experience' that always exceeds the 'facts', where, as concerns a reading of *Hamlet*, 'we should have to understand things which Shakespeare did not understand himself' ('*Hamlet*' [1919], *SP*, 49). This is not the statement of someone who expects annotation of literature to be particularly successful, as the personality and 'facts' that matter are located in the reading process, not the consciousness of the designing hand.

Dual responsibility for the final printed version of *The Waste Land* is not quite the same as an impersonal 'intention', the idea Eliot enshrined in 'Tradition and the Individual Talent' and which he extended into a definition of the exclusive poetic mind in both his essays on 'The Metaphysical Poets' and also in 'The Perfect Critic' (first published in *The Athenaeum*, 23 July 1920).[21] This latter was an enabling belief; the composition of poetry could be at one and the same time a fundamentally unknowable act (to both reader *and* writer), yet be as exact a procedure as in any scientific experiment. Note the description of the poet's mind as a catalytic 'shred of platinum' and 'a receptacle for seizing and storing up numberless feelings, phrases, images, which remain there until all the particles which can unite to form a new compound are present together' (*SP*, 41). Or the terms in which he regarded the expression of emotion in art: the search for an 'objective correlative', 'a set of objects, a situation, a chain of events which shall be the formula of that *particular* emotion' (*SP*, 48). The Poet creates by combining, and yet the conscious will of the individual artist is assigned a relatively diminished part to play, when you compare this emphasis to what may seem to be a similar formulation, in T.E. Hulme's *Speculations* (1924). There, the relationship of artist to material is one of continuous struggle, where the desire and urgency to get the personal truth expressed resembles an architect's duty to plan so exactly that her/his finished product is in no future danger of collapse. The 'exact curve' of the intention is what is required, which draws on a 'state of tension or concentration of mind' so intense that it demands an unrelenting 'grip over oneself' (Hulme 1924: 132–3). Here there is little room for Eliot's speculative scientist, whose knowledge of what his raw materials are capable of, those 'numberless feelings', is inevitably limited.

If we take Eliot's model of how the successful poem is put together as a reliable guide to our reading of *The Waste Land*, then we must regard it as an impassive object, a finished product that admits of no two ways of 'use' because its construction has been so singular and precise. Once found, a scientific formula will be faithfully followed to produce the original result. To carry the analogy further, a scientific formula can be learnt and is portable, its validity not limited to the circumstances of its immediate provenance. So too, we conclude, with the poem and its readers: no matter what the respective contexts of reader and writer are or may have been, there is a potential identity between the points of origin and reception, writerly intention and readerly experience. In this version of reading Eliot is at his most New Critical. There are abundant resemblances between this and, for example, the hopes for an 'objective' criticism in W.K. Wimsatt's *The Verbal Icon* (1970).[22]

We can perhaps see how the process by which *The Waste Land* made it to the public domain actually mirrors the critical principles Eliot espoused. Pound catalysed otherwise inert substance into life. Before we accept too readily Eliot's own account of how we are to read his work, though, we ought to summarize the assumptions on which these propositions are based. History does not touch the art object. Even the artist's identity is no reliable help in interpretation, as the self that is actually involved in the process of composition is not identical with the recordable self that leaves non-literary traces. *The Waste Land*, once constructed, is a self-sufficient structure, where, as is the case with a completed building, we have little further direct use to enquire into the architect's blueprint or as to where the construction company acquired their scaffolding. Perhaps by now this analogy may seem to be a little suspect. Does the process of reading resemble a form of disinterested contemplation? Texts are *verbal* entities and, while they may have been consciously designed and planned, they enter, and so engage with, another consciousness when read.

We might also look back at Eliot's own claim in his essays on the Metaphysicals and *Ulysses* that historical complexity visits indirectness on the writer. Presumably, the 'mythical method' would not be as urgent a requirement at another historical moment. There is also the consideration that, when he focused on the reader, Eliot allotted an independence, even a privileged insight, to interpretation; consider the essay on *Hamlet* and the passages in 'Tradition' where he found the best literary criticism to be self-critical. In this, Eliot anticipated much recent literary critical theory – in its emphasis both on a reader's response (see Steve Ellis's essay in this book) and on the writer's cultural role.

History and Culture in *The Waste Land*

> History has many cunning passages, contrived corridors
> And issues, deceives with whispering ambitions,
> Guides us by vanities . . .
>
> ('Gerontion' [1919, published in 1920], (CPP, 38)

This fickle donor disappoints humanity. The dead past, however, will not remain forgotten. Stetson's interred corpse has in fact been planted (ll. 69–76):

> What are the roots that clutch, what branches grow
> Out of this stony rubbish? Son of man,
> You cannot say, or guess, for you know only
> A heap of broken images, where the sun beats,
> And the dead tree gives no shelter, the cricket no relief . . .
>
> (WL, ll. 19–23)

In Freud's terminology, here there is the return of the repressed. In his study of Jensen's story, Gradiva, Freud saw the archaeologist, Norbert Hanold, as the type of self-absorbed humanity which searches for the new and finds it possesses the old: 'There is, in fact, no better analogy for repression, by which something in the mind is at once made inaccessible and preserved, than burial of the sort to which Pompeii fell a victim and from which it could emerge once more through the work of the spade' (Freud 1953, IX: 40). This interpenetration of past in the present collapses the historicity of what has occurred into our present understanding of it. Tradition is always effective, even when ignored.

The price of this is an effacement of the agencies by which particular histories are known and communicated. 'Impersonality' involves more than just the apparent disappearance of authorial personality to be replaced by art; it also evades the discontinuities that a detailed history might uncover. Better to outflank this by theoretical denial and metaphysical frames of reference than risk fragmentation, but if we return to the critical questions I started by posing, we might find routes into the work that are far from arbitrary. Is this an ordered work, or rather, one that *endorses* orderliness? This has been one of the questions that each contributor has addressed, perhaps not as a central issue, but as a concern that usually demands some form of address in criticism of the poem. We need to concentrate on the specific form of transcendence (or repression) that Eliot expresses, not merely as an object for description but as one for analysis.

One way of organizing the poem is to take as of central importance Eliot's note to line 218, the reference to Tiresias, 'though blind, throbbing between two lives'. His powers of prophecy deny the recording of individual historical events as a worthwhile guide to their truth: 'I Tiresias, old man with wrinkled dugs/Perceived the scene, and foretold the rest' (ll. 228–9). Eliot's note is complex. Tiresias, 'although a mere spectator and not indeed a "character", is yet the most important personage in the poem, uniting all the rest.' All males merge into one, just as 'all the women are one woman, and the two sexes meet in Tiresias'. His androgynous vision 'is the substance of the poem'. There then follows the relevant passage from *Metamorphoses* III, which is included not only to supply, as he puts it, 'anthropological interest', but also, we might suspect, to fill out the necessary space to justify the poem's individual publication. Tiresias is made to regard sex from both male and female experience, and, when he crosses Juno, he is blinded, earning the gift of prophecy as a recompense. To what does Tiresias refer, if not to a distinct 'character'? As Anthony Easthope points out, Tiresias does *not* narrate the whole poem. There are other distinct voices: Marie, the 'hyacinth' girl, Madame Sosostris, the cockney couple and three Thames-daughters. Substantially, though, the note does help us realize how much the reading experience of identifying multiple voices eventually becomes a *merging* of significance and not a progression towards some Grail: 'Clearly *The Waste Land* does not offer an objective context in which these impressions (scenes, voices) can be read as documentary report; each is intensively mediated through the speaker's consciousness to become what he thinks, remembers, wishes, imagines, fantasises' (Easthope 1983a: 333). The poem can exist as an expression of feeling without an origin, and yet its historical moment is not negligible, as it manages to be 'a general representation of modern experience', where its status as a product of a divided society is underlined by its defensive qualities, where it 'prevents the origin of its meaning coming into question and so, possible rejection' (Easthope 1983a: 343). Its success is a rhetorical one.

This attempt to do without a controlling centre to the poem is a perennial contemporary interest. For Ruth Nevo, the poem is most interesting in its determination to set up propositions only to dramatize, or involve the reader as witness to, their deconstruction (Nevo 1982). This reading is not greatly different from that of Calvin Bedient, although in summary his identification of a 'Protagonist' to the poem may seem a radical alternative. In practice, this 'voice' is so protean and multiple that it scarcely remains as a reference back to Eliot's conscious or unconscious self. It does identify the work as at one and the same time a most self-aware statement and also 'so other-conscious' (Bedient 1986: 221). We catch Eliot out in his evasions – deliberately – and we are thereby referred to some conception of the Absolute that stands clear of what we gradually perceive and experience as the mess of direct experience. By indirections we find direction out (Nevo with an intention added?).[23]

These alternatives are more closely allied than they would initially appear to be. They derive from a decision about Eliot's intention which takes him either to be fully aware of the tactical manoeuvres to which a reader will have to resort, or necessarily blind to its full effect because he is attuned to 'objective correlatives' and not a predicted reader's response. Given that the goal of these strains of criticism will be different, the reading process described is similar: we search for order and realize that that aim is either fallacious, if we only concentrate on the words on the page in their primary meanings, or intended, if we value the resort to the abstract ideas that exist only by way of hints and allusion.

When I dwelt on the allusions to *Our Mutual Friend* in Eliot's first draft and to Thomas Kyd in the closing lines it became clear how much was communicated in this way – not just by direct reference to a specific passage in a source text but by the associations that were unlocked in the process. The allusions and the route to such meanings (which may be down culs-de-sac as with several of Eliot's notes) enact a meaning that is only partly semantic, that is, translated from the source text and capable of paraphrase aside from the particular form of reading that has produced it. In Patricia Waugh's analysis of some continuities between Modernism and a more clearly relativistic postmodernism, Eliot's *desire* to establish connections between contingent appearances, to do without reason and yet also to locate some 'universal order' is everywhere evident, and that is the most enduring 'fact' about the poem and the reading process provoked by it (see Waugh 1992: 78–9).

The notion of such an order is of a stable ideal, the ghostly alternative to the rhetoric by which anarchy is expressed and so explored by the reader. But there is no clear decision behind this array of signifiers unless we intervene to create one and say that that was indeed what the poem (Eliot?) provoked us to do. In *Murder in the Cathedral* (1935) Eliot has Thomas Becket deny the usual division between agent and context in terms that seem very reminiscent of 'Tradition':

> Neither does the agent suffer
> Nor the patient act. But both are fixed
> In an eternal action, an eternal patience
> To which all must consent that it may be willed
> And which all must suffer that they may will it,
> That the pattern may subsist, for the pattern is the action
> And the suffering, that the wheel may turn and still
> Be forever still.
>
> (*CPP*, 245)

CHAPTER 1

The Politics of Redemption: Eliot and Benjamin

JOHN BOWEN

[Of all the intellectuals writing in the first great heyday of materialist criticism and cultural theory, it may be that Walter Benjamin, little known or regarded in his lifetime, will turn out out to be the one who speaks most eloquently to the contemporary sense of uncertainty, marginality and indeterminacy. Unlike his fellow-Marxists, Georg Lukács and Theodor Adorno, he had no 'system', no worked-out set of theoretical coordinates. Criticized by Adorno, among others, for its lack of theoretical consistency and rigour, his writing is oblique, allusive, gnomic. It seems to proceed by intuition and association as much as by logic, and its preferred mode is not the expository and argumentative favoured by the Marxist classics but the figurative and the allegorical. Where Lukács and the others, we might say, are 'realists', unshakeable in their assurance of the solidity of the real and the capacity of Marxism to comprehend and expound it, Benjamin is 'modernist', even, some would claim, 'postmodernist', in his fascination with the fragmentary, the eccentric and the trifling, the ephemeral detritus of the modern city. His work combines a poetic, visionary strain (betraying the influence of surrealism and of his lifelong interest in Jewish mysticism) with a sometimes breathtakingly abrupt recourse to the crude materiality of things, that *plumpes Denken* ('coarse thinking') recommended by his friend Brecht and described by Benjamin himself as 'nothing but the referral of theory to practice' (Benjamin 1970: 15).

This kind of thing struck his more orthodox Marxist friends as quite 'undialectical'; and just how heterodox it was becomes clear if we consider how little theoretical use he made of the central Marxist articulations of being/consciousness and base/superstructure. For Marxism, distancing itself sharply from the idealist philosophy which is one of its progenitors, our consciousness of the world and of ourselves, though inevitably the subjective starting-point of any understanding, is not in fact a primary reality at all, but a mental 'reflection' or representation, albeit a mediated and often distorted one, of the historical and material conditions in which we live, in a world shaped by historical forces and social conflicts ('class struggles') that proceed quite independent of and indifferent to our awareness of them.

This philosophical conception of the relation between consciousness and existence, which the French philosopher, Louis Althusser, called the 'epistemological break' that founded Marxism as a new form of critical knowledge, was developed in Marx's later writings into a sociological account of whole epochs or 'social formations', in which a foundation or 'base' of historically constituted social relations (between slaves and slave-owners, peasants and landowners, workers and employers) is represented to the human beings who live, inescapably and confusedly, within it as an ideological 'superstructure' of legal, philosophical, political and, not least, artistic activities 'in which men become conscious of the struggle and fight it out'. Thus the principal explanatory task, for a Marxist intellectual, is to explore the very complex relations or 'mediations' between a particular formation of the material base (the composition of antagonistic social forces at a given place and moment) and the manifestations of those fundamental conflicts in some region of the superstructure. Of course, Marxism aspires to be a good deal more than a contemplative theory of culture and society, and the political imperative for the Marxist intellectual, in contrast to those 'philosophers' who, in Marx's words, 'have been content so far to understand the world', must always be 'to change it'. But the success of the political project will always depend, he insisted, on the most rigorous pursuit of the theoretical one: to change the world, it is first of all necessary to understand it, in its full material and ideological historicity. Thus Marxism establishes a notably complex, 'dialectical' tension between theory and practice, contemplation and action.

Alongside more systematic theoreticians like Lukács and Adorno or, later, Jameson and Eagleton (see Eagleton 1976; Bloch et al. 1977; Jameson 1981), Benjamin's deployment of these fundamental notions looks metaphorical and improvisatory, and his unquestionable Marxist commitment has an ethical, at times an almost religious texture that owes more to what his friend Ernst Bloch called 'the principle of hope' than to any process of rigorous intellectual argument. It may be for that very reason that, as Marxism itself, along with all the other 'grand narratives' of modernity, falters in its historical stride and enters, once more, a period of profound self-scrutiny, the irresponsible flâneur Benjamin seems to have weathered better than some of his more confident and academically respectable contemporaries. More than any of the others, more even than his pupil and critic Adorno, he registered the terrible crisis of modernity represented by the rise of Hitler; and his secular pessimism drew him not to the well-upholstered realist fictions favoured by orthodox Marxism but to the decadent reveries of a Baudelaire, the glum allegorical obliquities of a Kafka, the mute, stricken gaze of Klee's Angel (see pp. 48–9). Political differences apart, his fractured, anguished vision makes his writings a vivid commentary on the early Eliot, the famous description of history as 'one single catastrophe which keeps piling wreckage upon wreckage' (Benjamin 1970: 259) recalling the poet's 'immense panorama of futility and anarchy which is contemporary history' (SP, 177). But although his suicide in 1940, while attempting to escape from Nazi-occupied Europe to rejoin his friends in the United States, shadows his all-too-brief existence with a tragic pathos, he remains in his writings an exemplar in the most difficult times of the secular 'principle of hope', and so, unlike the conservative (royalist, Anglo-Catholic) Eliot, soon to disparage the poem as mere 'rhythmical grumbling', holds open to later readers a radical and radically disconcerting Waste Land, haunted by the past, ravaged by the present, tormented by the possibility of change.]

TONY DAVIES

I

Who among us has not dreamed, in moments of ambition, of the miracle of a poetic prose, musical without rhythm and without rhyme, supple and staccato enough to adapt to the lyrical stirrings of the soul, the undulations of dreams and the sudden leaps of consciousness? This obsessive ideal is above all a child of our experience of great cities, of the intersecting of their myriad relations.[1]

This quotation links three writers who have explored in important ways how we think about writing in the modern world and the relationship between politics, society and literature. It comes from the dedication to Charles Baudelaire's book of prose poems, *Spleen de Paris*, and is a defining document within nineteenth-century French and European culture of the question of artistic modernity, and one which can still be used as a central reference in discussions of political and cultural freedom.[2] It is quoted by the German Jewish intellectual and critic, Walter Benjamin, in his great unfinished study of the Paris of the Second Empire and the work of Baudelaire, perhaps, even in its truncated form, the greatest Marxist study of literature and one of the most successful attempts to relate detailed historical analysis to literary criticism.

It is also a text of great relevance to the work of T.S. Eliot, the most important of all modern Anglo-American poets and critics. Eliot, like Baudelaire, was both fascinated and repelled by the experience of the city, and constantly explored in his early poetry the changes in the very fibres of human being and consciousness occasioned by the motor car, the telephone, the city street. His poetry, like Baudelaire's, is full of contemporary references and rhythms – like the Shakespeherean Rag in 'The Fire Sermon' (WL, l. 128) – behind which one can discern other more primitive and archaic forms and rituals. Both their writings seem to hold together in extreme tension conservative and radical impulses, lovingly attending to the debris of the modern world, finding in its melancholy ruins and violent eruptions the feeble traces of a lost order and the possibility of redemption.

Eliot was much influenced by Baudelaire and wrote about him on several occasions, as well as quoting Baudelaire's extraordinary address to the reader at the end of the opening section of The Waste Land: 'You! hypocrite lecteur! – mon semblable, – mon frère!'[3] The two writers share an interest in the relationship between abnormal states of mind, the experience of modern urban life and modes of modern writing. Baudelaire, like Eliot, is interested in the kinds of formal experimentation – the dissolving of the boundary between poetry and prose, lack of rhyme and rhythm, sudden juxtapositions – appropriate to the shock of new urban experiences. The well-regulated coherences of the bourgeois consciousness become prey to the dreams, ambitions and desires fostered by the city's inexplicable impositions:

> Fourmillante cité, cité pleine de rêves,
> Où le spectre en plein jour raccroche le passant.
>
> (CPP, 76)

It is with Benjamin, however, that we are more concerned, for Benjamin (like his friend and collaborator, Bertolt Brecht) wished to link such changes in social life and literary form to a political under-standing of the economic and class system in which they arise. To make such connections is one of the most difficult tasks that critics can set themselves, requiring not only the surest grasp of historical and textual detail, but also a more general method or theory to articulate or link them together. The dominant tradition within twentieth-century Anglo-American criticism has long resisted the linking of politics and literary criticism in this way, not least because of the influence of Eliot himself, whose own conservative critical tyranny was exercised under the suave mask of 'the common pursuit of true judgement' (SE, 25). For Eliot and for so many who have followed him, to try to relate, as

Benjamin does, a poet's *œuvre* to the society and economy, the life of the city and the people in which it appeared, is a task quixotic at best, malicious and absurd at worst.

Baudelaire's (and Benjamin's) quotation, then, is a way of putting *The Waste Land* in a new context, one in which questions of aesthetic form and practice lead out into questions of social and political form and practice, connections deeply resisted by the dominant institutional methods of literary criticism. Unfortunately, however, Benjamin's work on Baudelaire remains a fragment or set of fragments, never attaining the scale or completeness Benjamin intended. Like Eliot, Benjamin often reaches after a totalizing account, but is constantly arrested by the fragment. For this reason, it is better to approach *The Waste Land* not through Benjamin's more extended pieces of literary criticism on Baudelaire or seventeenth-century German tragic drama but through a briefer, more compact text, one of the most influential, if enigmatic, critical works of this century, his 'Theses on the Philosophy of History' (Benjamin 1970: 255–66).

The 'Theses', Benjamin's final piece of writing (apart from a short review), were completed in the spring of 1940. They are widely, almost universally, acknowledged to be of seminal importance: the German political philosopher, Jürgen Habermas, for example, took them as the natural starting point of his recent major study of philosophical and aesthetic modernity.[4] Like Eliot's poem, they have the riddling power of the great works of the creative imagination and are a text to which writers and critics are constantly drawn, uniting as they do a lucid and epigrammatic style with brevity and density of argument, addressing the central issues of twentieth-century history in urgent fragments of meditation.

The most striking thing about the 'Theses' is how different they are from what most people believe Marxist criticism to be. They look like a modernist text, forwarding their argument in fits and starts, through abrupt excisions and laconic epigrams. At key moments, they resort to curious visual images and metaphors, like that of the theological dwarf within the materialist automaton which opens the text. There is no attempt, as there is in many Marxist texts, either to be scientific in method or presentation, or to seduce or inspire through the power of rhetoric. The reader, like the stroller in the city, constantly meets jolts and shocks, 'a collage of images', in Richard Wolin's words, 'that kindles one's fascination, beseeches interpretation or decipherment' (Wolin 1982: xi).

For the reader of *The Waste Land*, the similarities between the two texts are immediately apparent, similarities of substance as well as of tone. They share a disgusted fascination with the confusion and degradation of contemporary society, and a desire and an inability to make coherent sense of it. Both are composed of uneasily overlapping and at times competing voices, mixing the resolutely secular with the mystically contemplative. The North American Marxist critic, Fredric Jameson, has written of Benjamin's work that it presents 'a vision of a world of ruins and fragments, an ancient chaos of whatever nature – these are some of the images that seem to recur, either in Benjamin himself or in your mind as you read him' (Jameson 1971: 61). As so often, a description of Benjamin could as easily be applied to Eliot. There are many coincidences and parallels in these two *œuvres*, constructed apparently in mutual ignorance, and which it is customary to see as belonging to very different histories.

They share a concern with time and change. I say 'time' rather than 'history', because the very term 'history' carries too many presuppositions that Eliot and Benjamin wished to reject. Time is central to the two texts, in many different ways: in the questioning of the obligations of the present to the texts of the past; in the interest in what stands outside or arrests the process of time; in the yearning the texts share for time to stand still and meaning to be self-present. Past, present and future meet in the obscure finds of esoteric research and the detritus of quotidian urban experience. Benjamin's presentation of the difficult necessity of reflection on the texts and events of the past for a politics determined to transform the future both resembles and extends the aesthetic practice of *The Waste Land*. Eliot's experiments with time are liable to be described as 'mythical', but are better thought of, as I shall show later, as allegorical.

This obligation to the past appears most strongly in the two writers' critical understanding, in the citation and quotation that is so central a part of their writing. First-time readers of *The Waste Land* are often confused by the sheer weight of quotations, allusions and references in it. Eliot, like Benjamin, was fascinated by what Marx called 'the tradition of the dead generations [which] weighs like a nightmare on the brains of the living',[5] by the sense that the modern author is condemned merely to reproduce fragments of past achievement, to be not an artist building his or her own epic or monument but a mere *bricoleur*, fadging together the spare parts of dead discourses, painfully elaborating the most complex of structures to carry out the simplest of tasks, Heath Robinson not Michelangelo. Both responded to this through an art of montage, juxtaposing stolen fragments in unlikely combinations, filching and paying a debt in the same ambiguous gestures.

Both these urban, deracinated intellectuals, who produced their greatest work between the First and Second World Wars, were concerned with the relation of past and present, particularly the culture and literature of the past, to an apparently empty and chaotic world that ignored or despised its history. Both found their greatest objects of critical interest in the work of seventeenth-century and some nineteenth-century French writers. But their fates were very different: one died honoured and full of years, the recipient of a Nobel prize and the Order of Merit, the other a hasty suicide in flight from the Gestapo. And similar loves and needs took them to very different political allegiances: one to Marxism, the other to a royalist conservatism. They share a view of history which emphasizes the partial and the heterogeneous over the progressive and totalizing, and are both more concerned with suffering and redemption than enlightenment and triumph. Benjamin's modernist Marxism leads him, however, to a very different understanding of the causes of that suffering and the nature of that redemption.

II

A German Jew, born in 1892, Benjamin witnessed the trauma of the First World War and the uncertainties of the Weimar Republic, before fleeing the Nazi dictatorship. Like Eliot he was an exile for many years, in France and elsewhere, never holding an academic post or enjoying a regular income, but producing in his curtailed and harried life penetrating and fertile analyses of both esoteric historical topics and contemporary culture. Unlike Eliot, whose political response to the interwar crisis became increasingly repressive and authoritarian, he was drawn to socialist politics, becoming an intimate friend of the German Marxist playwright, Bertolt Brecht.

Benjamin's influence in literary and cultural criticism has been enormous over recent years, in part because of the extraordinary intellectual energy that comes from a mind that holds together such disparate fields as Jewish mysticism and socialist politics, seventeenth-century melancholy and the invention of photography, and in part from the restless reflection of modern experience and modernist writing in the very textures of his prose. His was a mind that could produce great essays on both avant-garde and scholarly literary topics and yet also sought to grasp the very currents of contemporary change in the minutiae of daily life in Naples, Moscow and his native Berlin. His essays include philosophical reflections on the nature of language, on smoking hashish in Marseilles, on surrealism and on book-collecting as well as literary studies of Kafka, Proust and Brecht. His work holds in occluded tension many of the contradictions that recur in the lives of socialist intellectuals, as it registers the urgent and conflicting demands of contemporary suffering and scholarly discipline.

The reason for this success stems in large part from the sheer intellectual quality of his writings. One needs only to compare the work of his socialist contemporaries in England such as Christopher Caudwell and Stephen Spender to realize how acutely Benjamin read the signs of the times and how presciently he anticipated contemporary cultural debate. His posthumous star has continued to rise within academic literary criticism for Marxists and deconstructionists alike. The 'Theses' have a unique status in this *œuvre*, because of their generality, their (disputed) status as a 'final testament', and their difficult relationship of recapitulation, extension and revision of his earlier work. For many they have been seen as the 'flagship' or the 'crowning testament' of Benjamin's work, but for others they represent a confused and unfinished retreat from his earlier, better writing, a sad capitulation to the forces that were so shortly to press him to death.[6]

Benjamin writes at what may have been the nadir of twentieth-century European history. The Nazi–Soviet non-aggression pact seemed to most Marxists the very worst betrayal of the hopes of the October revolution. The contrast between this and the optimism of a mere two decades before, when the Bolshevik victory seemed about to be followed by successor revolutions in Germany and elsewhere, was immense. The German workers' movement, the best-organized and most powerful in Europe, had capitulated without a fight to the Nazis, who in the dark days of 1940 seemed to carry all before them. The tone of the 'Theses' is very near despair, as Benjamin attempts to comprehend the failure of so many of the decade's 'clever hopes'[7] and to begin to hope again. This despair was a general one, but we can again contrast Benjamin's continuing allegiance to socialism with his left-wing English contemporaries, most of whom were at that moment in full-scale retreat from political militancy to conservative quietism.

In attempting in the 'Theses' to explain this unprecedented disaster, Benjamin sees the political failure of the Left in Germany as being caused by a fundamentally flawed view of human history, which has disastrous political consequences. He criticizes the Left's – historicist – view of temporal change and attempts to think of alternative methods of relating historical understanding to political action. The question of history is a central one for socialists; Marxism defines itself as a *historical* material-ism. Benjamin believed that this concern has too often translated itself into a simple belief in progress. There has been little exploration of *time*, that most difficult of subjects, within the socialist tradition, where attempts to question common-sense notions of time are often simply dismissed. Socialists have in particular usually rejected attempts to speak of moments outside or arresting of time as being necessarily trans-historical, idealist or theological, as they have rejected a concern with the instantaneous, the fashionable and the mystical. In short, Marxist theories of history have too often mirrored the grounding assumptions of bourgeois academic history, both neglecting the profound transform-ations in temporal experiences engendered by capitalism and forgetting how strange and mysterious time itself is.

Those who have written about the consciousness of time in modern life have often been led to the same conclusion – that the modern world creates, on the one hand, the empty time characterized by the clock-card and the production line, and, on the other, the unprecedented possibilities of novelty and transformation once the customs of tradition begin to be questioned. History is no neutral professional activity to be left to specialists in such a world. Like the Marx of *The Eighteenth Brumaire of Louis Bonaparte*, a text that lies closely behind the 'Theses', Benjamin seeks for a practice of writing that can think the forces of con-tinuity and novelty, of infinite hope for the future and total regression to barbarism, that fill the contemporary crisis with danger and oppor-tunity, and where the paradoxical novelty of the age is found in Fascism's brutal archaism.

For this reason the 'Theses' are profoundly concerned with time, both its nature and how the human subject comprehends the past and looks to the future. For Benjamin, as for many of the greatest modern thinkers, it is necessary to recharge human consciousness with a radical awareness of time and temporal change, which many orthodox forms of historical knowledge and history writing actively prevent. Many historians try to make the past familar to us; Benjamin wanted to make our own times unfamiliar, just as literary modernists sought to 'make strange' conventional forms of perception and understanding.

Much of the success and novelty of capitalist production depends on its ability to reorganize time in significantly new ways. The most representative of these changes was the creation by Henry Ford and Frederick Taylor of modern production-line methods, which empty labour of its meaning through the routinization, standardization and repetition of simple tasks. Such changes institutionalize a profound and unbridgeable divide between dreary conformity to the sterile demands of external clock-time and the inexpressibility of sudden intensities of subjective desire. At the same time as production is routinized, the development of new and more intense modes of consumption demands speed, surprise and shock in its colonization of desire, encouraging the abrupt irruption of discontinuities within customary life. It becomes more difficult to maintain the traditional coherence of subjective memory and desire; empty repetition and random contingency jostle next to infinite hope and subjective possibility.

For Benjamin, Marxism's claim to be able, for the first time in human history, to envisage the necessary conditions of a world of free self-determined individuals marks a profound break with all previous theories and methods of historical understanding, of which the most powerful and dangerous is that of 'progress', the belief that there is a pattern to human history of steady improvement. The idea of progress was influential in the Enlightenment and given added impetus by the technological revolutions of the nineteenth century. There are various inflections of this powerful ideology: progress through moral improvement, natural selection or technological development, for example. All these 'historicist' beliefs are for Benjamin inadequate to the continuing crises of this century's history, fitting as they so easily do into the most familiar economic and social structures of capitalism – the wage-packet, the lure of the commodity and the relentless search for new markets and greater 'efficiency'. Within socialist thought, a commitment to 'progress' marks a caesura between evolutionary and revolutionary versions of political change. If one believes that things will, of themselves, improve, then the need for revolutionary struggle is diminished. A faith in progress leads to a complacent understanding of Fascism and capitalism alike.

'Historicism', the dominant academic form of history-writing and the view of history that underpins social democracy, is Benjamin's immediate target. His contempt is fierce:

> The politicians' stubborn faith in progress . . . and . . . their servile integration in an uncontrollable apparatus have been . . . aspects of the same thing . . . Nothing has corrupted the German working class so much as the notion that it was moving with the current.
>
> (Benjamin 1970: 260)

Benjamin is not rejecting the rational analysis of history here, for he shares other Marxist critics' belief in causal understanding of historical change as the most important demystified understanding of the world.

But for Benjamin, the danger is that such analyses are neither revolutionary nor philosophical enough, complacently orientated to the future in a way that is incompatible with radical action in the present, subsuming its infinite possibilities into the conformity of slowly unwinding stories. The political consequences of this are disastrous:

> Social democracy thought fit to assign to the working class the role of the redeemer of future generations, in this way cutting the sinews of its greatest strength. This training made the working class forget both its hatred and its spirit of sacrifice, for both are nourished by the image of enslaved ancestors rather than that of liberated grandchildren.
>
> (Benjamin 1970: 262)

Against this progressivist, linear view of history, which seemed so deeply engrained within orthodox academic practice, common sense and political strategy alike, Benjamin invokes the fruit of both recherché scholarship and modernist artistic experiment, a characteristic mixture of backward and forward glances. Against the windless enclosure of 'homogeneous, empty time', Benjamin invokes the *Jetztzeit* – the 'time filled with the presence of the now' (Benjamin 1970: 263). This important, difficult concept has its origin in Jewish mysticism, but in the essay represents the possibility within any moment to bring with it the most revolutionary break with its predecessors. In illustration, Benjamin tells the anecdote of the French Revolution in which the church clocks of Paris were spontaneously shot at, showing the desire within any truly revolutionary moment to mark a break with the past to suspend the present and so command the future (Benjamin 1970: 264).

This leads to a very different conception of intellectual practice, one appropriate to the disturbed and revolutionary times in which he lived. The critic is like a guerrilla, her task 'to wrest tradition away from a conformism that is about to overpower it' (Benjamin 1970: 257). The past is not 'there', waiting to be discovered and revealed in the patient accumulation of detail, but appears at moments of crisis in fleeting, fragmentary form:

> For every image of the past that is not recognised by the present as one of its own concerns threatens to disappear irretrievably . . . To articulate the past historically does not mean to recognise it 'the way it really was' . . . It means to seize hold of a memory as it flashes up at a moment of danger.
>
> (Benjamin 1970: 257)

Benjamin is here rejecting narrative in favour of the image, revitalizing the use of the past by a practice of writing simultaneously more philosophical and more aesthetic. The critic makes a 'tiger's leap' into the past (Benjamin 1970: 263), approaching historical material only when it offers 'a revolutionary chance in the fight for the oppressed past' (Benjamin 1970: 265).

Eliot's earlier poetry is full of concern with time. In 'Rhapsody on a Windy Night' the empty repetition of clock-time ('Twelve o'clock . . . Half-past one . . . Half-past two . . . Half-past three') is as regular as it is meaningless (*CPP*, 24–5). Subjective time, by contrast, experienced as memory, is full of meaning, but randomly and terrifyingly so:

> Midnight shakes the memory
> As a madman shakes a dead geranium.
>
> (*CPP*, 24)

But it is only in *The Waste Land* that this comes to have a properly historical dimension, in which Eliot is concerned with the fate of a civilization as well as an individual. Like Benjamin, he found it hard to look at the present with any equanimity or the future with any hope. He, too, distrusted the ideology of progress and felt that so many of the customary forms of writing verse were complicit with it. Instead of telling a story, he accumulates significant fragments by which the crimes and violence of the past survive in the present.

History in Eliot's verse exists in traces, shot through with pain and unease, which briefly flash into enigmatic existence at a moment of danger. After the rapes of the Thames-daughters, the voice of St Augustine – 'To Carthage then I came' (l. 307) – forces itself into the poem's consciousness; the sight of the hooded hordes is followed by the falling towers of 'Jerusalem Athens Alexandria' (l. 374); rumours 'Revive for a moment a broken Coriolanus' (l. 416). Time seems meaningful only for the briefest instant, as when suddenly, out of the disjointed parts, a moment crystallizes outside time, charged with enigmatic power and significance:

> – Yet when we came back, late, from the hyacinth garden,
> Your arms full, and your hair wet, I could not
> Speak, and my eyes failed, I was neither
> Living nor dead, and I knew nothing,
> Looking into the heart of light, the silence.
>
> (ll. 37–41)

Benjamin calls his method of writing 'literary montage', linking it to the experiments of Soviet revolutionary cinema, but it is also very close to Eliot's technique. Like Benjamin, Eliot recounts events 'without distinguishing between major and minor ones' (Benjamin 1970: 256), attempting to find a mode of writing that can 'wrest tradition away from a conformism that is about to overwhelm it' (Benjamin 1970: 257), finding Dante's *Inferno* on London Bridge (l. 63) and ending a night at the pub with the words of Ophelia (l. 172). The writer receives the past in fragments, often quotations, which come together in a unity that is like (to use one of Benjamin's favourite metaphors) a constellation. Despair at the waste land of the present is alleviated by utopian moments which seem to anticipate a redeemed future in which time is full of meaning.

It is this last concern that makes the two writers so interested in cultural history. What, asks Benjamin, is the critic to make of the weight of cultural treasure that the present receives from the past, and what relationship can it have to the suffering and exploitation out of which it was forced and which presses so urgently in the present? This is a difficult and continuing question, and there are various easy, inadequate answers to it. The past, or an idealized version of it, for example, has often been thought the safest place to hide from the suffering of the present. Alternatively, the past has been presented as the 'tradition' or 'heritage' of a country, emptying it of contradiction and conflict and allying it with the interests of the rich and powerful. Nothing could be further from the spirit of these two texts, for both had a sense of the value but also the profound ambiguities of the cultural treasures of the past, which in *The Waste Land* speak of rape, of violence, of loss and emptiness, and which for Benjamin were documents of barbarism as much as of civilization (Benjamin 1970: 258). This unwillingness to see the past as either a refuge or an irrelevance is the most difficult part of their legacy to assimilate, and their continuing challenge.

These writers, then, share two things: the belief that the authentic apprehension of time and history requires in the contemporary crisis the interrogation of fragments; and the conviction that cultural history requires both a deep obligation to the past and a recognition of the barbarism that it bears with it. Holding the pathos of temporal finitude with the scent of the fashionably new brings Benjamin at his closest to Eliot. Like the courtiers and tyrants in Eliot's beloved Renaissance playwrights and Benjamin's seventeenth-century tragedians, they meditate on finery and skulls and the space between them, in societies on the very edge of anarchy. The importance of using Benjamin in understanding

Eliot is not simply to find a more radical reading of a poem. The twentieth century has faced in myths of tradition and national identity some of the most powerful threats to its dreams of social freedom and enlightenment.

III

The Waste Land is full of different things, and juxtaposes and rearranges the most radically different materials seized from widely different places, times and cultures. The reader moves back and forth between scenes of suffering and despair. There are glimpses and echoes of past beauty, but like the Cleopatra figure (ll. 77ff.) such beauty and art is deceptive and troubling. Time itself is troubled, hangs heavy, is paradoxical or mechanical, and nothing connects with nothing. There is a constant vague hope of some redeeming force appearing, although it is unclear what that might be. Like certain kinds of film, the poem proceeds by rapid cutting and instantaneous shifts in space and time. We move in seconds from Margate Sands to Carthage, and from the Fisher King via the Prince of Aquitaine to the mad Hieronymo avenging his son. One is constantly jostled, seemingly at random, by quotations, by the random shocks of enigmatic faces and voices. Only glimpses remain of a lost fusion of public and private time and meaning in the passage of Elizabeth and Leicester down the Thames (ll. 279ff.) and the allusions to the Grail quest. The modern interpenetrates the ancient as Tiresias surveys the typist and the contingencies of everyday life erupt within the work of art.

In reading commentators on this strange and disturbing text one often feels that sensibilities very alien to Eliot's are attempting to comprehend it and, in doing so, to neutralize much of its radicalism and shock value. Critics committed to the values of coherence, order and temporal continuity immediately begin to tidy up the mess. They assimilate its broken structure to a coherent whole by reducing it to a symptom of its history or postulating an essence or unifying consciousness behind it, sweeping away its abortions and used contraceptives,[8] shoring up its ruins once more. The simplest version of this failure to read the poem is the response of the contemporary critic who saw Eliot as a drunken helot,[9] but it is present in much more sophisticated readers such as F.R. Leavis who claimed that the poem is 'the product of an inclusive consciousness'[10]. It is, of course, part of the process of making a text into a monument to claim a unity in this way, but the 'centres' to the poem discovered by critics rarely coincide: Tiresias, the hyacinth girl, Madame Sosostris's table, all have been taken, with equal arbitrariness, as the heart of the poem.[11]

In Benjamin's work, we have a critical text of equal strangeness and disruptive force, committed not to finding coherence, unity and structure where none at first appear, but to grasping in a radical way the nature of temporality and fragmentation, and the causes of ruin and pain. It makes no assumption that the finding of meaning in the modern world is an easy or natural affair. Equally fascinated by history, equally unwilling to organize that interest into a coherent pattern or narrative, Eliot and Benjamin share the belief not that the catastrophe is about to occur, but that it has already happened. To live through such a crisis where all previous fixed points and coherences seem to collapse requires suspicion of all unified forms of historical narrative and explanation, any form of writing that does not register in its very fabric the marks of loss, pain and fragmentation.

Time presses hard in *The Waste Land*, and causes much bafflement to its readers, frustrating most of our hopes and assumptions about how poems organize themselves. The poem, like the spring, mixes memory and desire, impelling its characters and readers backward in time to recuperate the past into the present, and forward to the fulfilment of desire and the resolution of enigma. Complex patterns of progress and regression, repetition and irruption, resist at each moment the reduction of such flux to pattern, argument or progress. Temporal indicators – autumn, spring, in the winter, a year ago – are constantly invoked and yet remain unassimilable to any unified field. Desire is uncertain and deceptive, memory disconnected and fragmentary, breaking on the rocks of repetition, uncertainty and death. In this flux of relativities without a constant, the notion of 'progress' in human affairs or stories is rejected at root. Time's stumps wither.

The opening of *The Waste Land* is familiar but strange. Eliot confounds together the human and vegetable, as lilacs breed (or are bred), snow is forgetful and April cruel. Winter kept us warm, we are told, but we do not know how, or even who 'we' are, whether eaters of dried tubers or the tubers themselves. The poem moves forward through temporal markers – 'Winter kept us warm . . . Summer surprised us' (ll. 5, 8) – but it is impossible to assimilate the statements to a single place or coherent story. Is there a contrast to be drawn between being kept warm and being surprised by a season, or are we expected to infer a causal relation? Such strangeness is endemic to the poem and to Eliot's art, which constantly tampers with conventional phrasing to create a syntax capable, like cubist painting, of holding together very different perceptions of space and time: a man called Stetson at Mylae (ll. 69–70); fishmen (l. 263); dead souls on London Bridge (ll. 62–3); sprouting corpses (ll. 71–2); a chuckle (not a grin) which spreads 'from ear to ear' (l. 186).

Behind the chaos, it has often been thought, lies coherence. For the Italian Marxist, Franco Moretti, for example, *The Waste Land* contains 'an essentially mythical view of history' for 'on the one hand it makes history seem an accumulation of debris; on the other it presents mythic structure as a point of suspension and reorganisation of this endless fugue' (Moretti 1983: 222). For Moretti, Eliot, in a deeply conservative way, is throwing away the possibility of understanding the world in a rational and causative manner by postulating a transcendent or suprahistorical patterning which lies behind or beneath merely human history and by which the poem is organized. There is for Moretti a 'radical devaluation of history' in *The Waste Land* which is engaged in

> overturning the very way in which Western civilisation has considered the historical process. History must no longer be seen as irreversible as regards the past, and mainly unpredictable as regards the future, but as a cyclical mechanism which is . . . fundamentally static; it lacks a truly temporal dimension.
>
> (Moretti 1983: 222)

Georg Lukács, perhaps the most important of all Marxist aestheticians this century, was equally hostile to any attempt to suspend or interrupt the achievements of secular realism through any concessions to the use of myth. This led him to reject, for example, James Joyce's *Ulysses* (which draws constant parallels between the world of Homeric legend and contemporary Dublin) and to champion against modernist innovation figures such as Thomas Mann, who were for him the true heirs of the fictional achievements of the nineteenth-century bourgeoisie.[12] Myth entails for these writers a fundamentally static understanding of the world which robs the present of any possibility of radical change or the seizing by humanity of its own history, and condemns them to a field of force without aim or direction. There is, for Moretti as for Lukács, a choice between an essentially demystified secular narrative and a mystifying conservative mythicism. *The Waste Land* in such an account is firmly part of the latter.

One must suspect that any reading that sees *The Waste Land* as static must be flawed, and Benjamin can help us to see why. Clearly there is mythical material in the poem, but if there really were a 'single and immutable structure' to the poem, it would be possible to demonstrate it. This has never been successfully accomplished, and Moretti simply presupposes what he ought to show when he claims that Madame Sosostris's table is at the centre of the poem. Generally, he pays more attention to the poem's Notes and Eliot's essay on Joyce, and in doing so shows the danger of taking the critical word for the creative deed. The feeling (confirmed by the decades of exegesis) that the poem does not in fact have the coherence and unity we expect of myth is also backed up by what we know of the poem's composition. Eliot handed Ezra Pound a bunch of drafts and fragments and Pound handed back a smaller one, *The Waste Land* as we know it. Eliot, rather desperately, does say in the Notes that we are supposed to think that the poem is all seen through Tiresias's consciousness (*CPP*, 78), but to psychologize myth in this way is already to admit defeat. If Eliot really did attempt systematic analogies in imitation of Joyce, then we can only say that he made a very hamfisted job of it. There are many opportunistic parallels, but no more.

Of course if you argue, as I am doing, that the poem does not have a coherent mythical structure underlying it, then it is natural to ask what coherence the poem does have. Benjamin, and the Marxist tradition behind him, can help us with this. For Marx one of the most distinctive things about modern society is its transformation of all things into commodities, and Benjamin tries to see the aesthetic consequences of this fact for modern art and modernism. The writer traditionally is supposed to write in significant ways about significant things. What happens, he asks, when everything is transformed into a commodity, when all use value becomes simply exchange value? One response, of course, is to find those things that have not been commodified in this way: death and suffering, for example (neither of which is likely to be on sale at Sainsbury's), religious faith or the recesses of the unconscious or nature. We can see all these strategies in literary modernism, most notably in the work of Beckett and Proust, and quite a lot of them in Eliot's work which continually returns to such subject-matter. But he also attempts to use the freedom of the commodity for purposes very alien to it, purposes which Benjamin calls allegorical.

Allegory might seem the most recherché of literary topics, the province perhaps of annotators of *The Faerie Queene*. With characteristic surprise, Benjamin sees it as peculiarly *modern*, belonging to societies in which things are stripped of intrinsic meaning. Such, he argues, is overwhelmingly the case in the devalued world of the commodity of modern capitalist society. If an advertising executive can arbitrarily associate a snatch of Puccini or a fluffy dog with a car or a toilet roll, then so, too, can the modernist writer, albeit for very different ends. 'Allegory', Fredric Jameson argues, 'is precisely the dominant mode of expression of a world in which things have for whatever reason been sundered from meanings, from spirit, from genuine human existence' (Jameson 1971: 71). The world that we live in is, for Benjamin, a ruined one whose literary forms reflect that ruined condition in their very texture.

This helps us cut through the dilemma of unity and/or fragmentation, by displacing a purely formal question into a formal-historical one, and pointing to the allegorical role of the text in such a society. *The Waste Land* neither has the 'organic' or plantlike unity often claimed for poetry since the Romantics, nor the coherence of mythical plot or structure. Its parts have the unity of stars in a constellation perhaps, or the archaeological coherence of a ruined and much rebuilt city; like Schliemann's Troy, the poem is a ruin of a ruin, comprising treasures and detritus, glittering jewels and broken potsherds scattered on a plain, the remnants of a lost civilization destroyed in flames. It is this that gives *The Waste Land* its historical importance: its willingness to remain a ruin and not seek to become a monument. Of course, critics have ever since attempted to rebuild the city, but have continued to fail.

For although (as academic critics are only too willing to point out) *The Waste Land* is a deeply cultured poem, requiring similarly cultured readers to understand its finer points, it is not a celebration of Western culture but its obituary, a catalogue not of treasures but of horrors, a black museum of madness, rape and destruction. The poem is fascinated by the spectacle of dead or dying civilizations, and all the major empires of Europe figure in the poem: the Austro-Hungarian in the figure of Marie in 'The Burial of the Dead' (ll. 13–16); the Ottoman through the Smyrna merchant (l. 209); the Russian in the 'hooded hordes' (l. 368) and the British in the constant invocations of a London on the edge of collapse. Each appears at a 'moment of danger' in the poem, whether sexual, social or political. The Smyrna merchant offers a dirty weekend in Brighton; Marie must hold tight not to fall; the hooded hordes swarm 'over endless plains, stumbling in cracked earth'; London Bridge is falling down. Tiny fragments invoke civilizations indistinguishable from barbarism, then disappear into the silence that surrounds them.

There is, though, a strong temptation for the reader to try to find a coherent system underlying the poem. If there is nothing holding the bits together, one might feel, there is not much point in going on. In a world where everything seems totally stripped of significance, we need at least a hope of it all making sense one day. This seems the right response to the poem, although increasingly one comes to realize that the text will not give us that coherence. It is this, perhaps, that makes the poem the least nostalgic in the language, constantly pushing us forward but gradually and at the same time teaching that any revelation is not going to come from a book.

This is not necessarily a socialist idea, but it is perhaps the preliminary to one, and makes the poem a good deal more open to history and radical in its consequences than we are often asked to believe. To read a text like *The Waste Land*, then, might provide a model for how the socialist might read history, no longer attempting to tell 'the sequence of events like the beads of a rosary' (Benjamin 1970: 265) but grasping the past 'as an image which flashes up at the instant when it can be recognised' (Benjamin 1970: 257). To do so is to come to terms with the strangeness of time, and the inadequacy of most of our conceptions of it, and to be able to live in a crisis where all previous fixed points and coherences seem to collapse. We recognize in Eliot a suspicion, akin to Benjamin's, of historicism, seeing in it an impoverishment of our relationship to history and memory; a divorce between past and present; an inability to comprehend the particular kind of knowledge that art can give us; a loss of ability to understand time before the final two seconds that is human history in the twenty-four hours of the history of the universe; a weak notion of the present-as-transition and the possibilities embedded within it; little sense of existential pain and suffering. Benjamin once described Baudelaire as a 'secret agent' (Wolin 1982: 230) in the enemy camp, an agent of the secret discontent of his own class with its own rule. The same is true of Eliot.

IV

During the modern period, the relation of the past to the present has been as difficult as it has been important. For students of English the relationship between the texts of the past, in idioms and forms often deeply historically outmoded, and a society that for the most part is happy to ignore them, is a continuing and urgent problem. It is also the most acute of questions for Marxists, one of whose central concerns is the need to explain in historical terms a contemporary society seemingly dedicated to the shedding of such understandings. Eliot and Benjamin offer characteristically modernist replies: in Eliot the irruption within history of the throbbing intensities of subjective guilt and desire; in Benjamin the refashioning of the most recalcitrant and forgotten material into the matter of revolutionary thought.

Their solutions might appear less radical now, in what is often referred to as the 'postmodern' era, when forms of disjunction and *bricolage* are common enough and the average pop video has as many temporal leaps and spatial jumps as *The Waste Land*. In the cultural changes of the last half-century, it might be said, what was once pioneering has become simply another style, mixing personal anecdote and vaguely apocalyptical mutterings, the merest staple of quotidian media imagery. Its form is now commonplace; the simultaneity of the non-simultaneous will not delay the children of the media age too long. Such an argument has the advantage of seeming both effortless and radical, and should for that reason be treated with caution. It is true that forms of *bricolage* and historical quotation are common enough today in the grab-bags of postmodernism. But what is equally common is their studied removal of conflict, and the consequent poverty of their cognitive and critical ability. Much less assimilable to this world are the pain and suffering that are linked, of necessity, in Benjamin's and Eliot's work to knowledge of the past and change in the present.

This is best seen in perhaps the single most important image of the 'Theses', where Benjamin invokes the angel of history, who 'sees one single catastrophe which keeps piling wreckage upon wreckage and hurls it in front of his feet' (Benjamin 1970: 259). Unable to help, unable to withdraw his gaze, the angel can only open his mouth in vain as he is swept backwards towards the future. There is no better description of the effect of *The Waste Land* on the reader. All historical perspective that causal, linear narrative permits us, disappears in the poem. All knowledge comes too late. Tight against the front of the picture plane, the resolute surface of the poem admits no consolatory depths or explanations. No recession, no subordination, no hierarchy of major and minor figures is permitted as we are propelled through the poem. Like the angel, the reader sees in human history and culture no chain of events but a single catastrophe piling rubble upon rubble.

Indeed, Benjamin's angel has many similarities both to the Sybil of the epigraph to *The Waste Land* and to Tiresias, 'the most important personage in the poem' (*CPP*, 78). Tiresias can move within time but sees only the same repetitive exploitation wherever he is:

(And I Tiresias have foresuffered all
Enacted on this same divan or bed;
I who have sat by Thebes below the wall
And walked among the lowest of the dead.)

(*WL*, ll. 243–6)

The Sybil, unlike Tiresias, can see but not move, sharing with him and with Benjamin's angel the fate of living within and outside time simultaneously. Hanging in a cage, unable to die, she looks into the future but can do nothing to change or alter it. Like the angel, she suffers the pain of witnessing human events while being unable to participate in them, segregated by a knowledge which is experienced only as suffering, seeing only a chaos of enigmatic fragments in the passage of human history. The angel can gaze open-mouthed at the accumulation of horrors which it witnesses; the Sybil wishes only to die (*CPP*, 59).

To say that the strength or importance of a text rests in its ability to fill the reader with despair, to make the spectacle of suffering an experience of it, is, of course, a dangerous argument, not because it might forestall the notion that all texts are as easy and pleasurable to scan as the latest magazine, but because there seems to lie within it something that at root seems hostile to the meaning and hope of socialism, the possibility for the first time in human history of a society where those who work also own and control the fruits of their labours. And indeed, it is here that so many socialists turn away from *The Waste Land*, and perhaps Benjamin's 'Theses', too. At this point, it is said, despite all the admiration we have for these two texts, despite all their radicalism, their innovation, their lapidary brilliance, there is a parting of the ways. A view of human history that denies all possibility of analysis, of understanding and of collective willed action, is simply irreconcilable on any level with a belief in socialism. It is no longer a questioning of progress, but a force in opposition to it. Such despair, these readers would argue, only unbends the springs of action; it becomes a symptom not a diagnosis. The kind of pessimism that Benjamin and Eliot share is precisely the wrong response to this century's catastrophes, inaccurate and generalizing in its history, quiescent and self-defeating in its politics. The task of the socialist critic is to tap the resources of hope, not to eat the bread of despair.

Now this seems to me wrong, but it is a serious point, and it may explain why some good critics have pointed to the similarities of tone and temperament between Eliot and Benjamin, and then taken the argument no further. It is certainly puzzling how such similar ideas of time and history can have such different political conclusions as Eliot's conservatism and Benjamin's Marxism. Perhaps it is silly to compare a quasi-philosophical essay with a poem, but the problem may well be bigger than this, pointing to something quite significant about literature and politics in the twentieth century. It appears in the way that, in both Eliot and Benjamin, writing and redemption are linked.

The Waste Land is full of desire for change; it sees a world of brutality and chaos which it yearns to redeem: 'Shall I at least set my lands in order?' (l. 425). In the end, though, the poem absorbs these desires into the quiescent and passive ethic of suffering and acceptance represented by its final words, an essentially subjective calm within the storm of fragmented languages. At first it may seem as if Benjamin has fallen prey to similar feelings, as he, too, uses an apparently religious vocabulary of redemption to withstand the chaotic violence of society and history. But in fact he is again using a religious vocabulary for thoroughly secular purposes, introducing the theme of redemption in the second of the 'Theses' for very different reasons. Because, he argues, we can only love or find happiness in the world we know, and among the people we have met in our time and place, 'our image of happiness is indissolubly bound up with the image of redemption' (Benjamin 1970: 256).

This seems at first a puzzling thing for a Marxist to say, but only if we assume that redemption is a mainly religious matter. It is, however, a word of secular origin: according to the *Shorter Oxford English Dictionary*, to 'redeem' means simultaneously to 'free, deliver and restore', in particular to 'free from economic bondage'. It is thus for Benjamin a more ample and generous concept for socialists than that of 'freedom' or 'liberation', embracing not just the liberation of present and future generations, but the justifying, and indeed the avenging, of the exploited dead; 'the image of enslaved ancestors' is for the working-class movement 'the sinews of its greatest strength' (Benjamin 1970: 262). The offence has already happened, and is continuing to be committed; redemption, in this secular sense, carries with it the memory of exploitation, which 'liberation' and 'progress', turned to the future, forget. To reject the idea of progress is not to reject the idea of liberation, but to amplify it.

Benjamin then goes on to complicate the matter, again using a religious vocabulary, by introducing the theme of the claims of the dead upon us, arguing that we have for them a 'Messianic' power (Benjamin 1970: 256). A messiah is, of course, someone who ends history as we know it and liberates the dead, but it seems a curious thing to say, and a long way removed from what we usually think of as a socialist idea. Surely, it might be said, the whole point of a socialist society is that things are simply better – more just, more democratic, less exploitative? What is the point of dragging in a religious vocabulary to such secular concerns? We cannot, of course, in a literal sense rescue the dead, or prevent their exploitation and suffering, but we can in another way. There is today great wealth and great poverty in the world; these divisions are historical and we recognize in them the reproduction of wealth, fortune and class identity over generations and centuries. Such wealth belongs to those who created it, and to speak of redemption is to acknowledge that debt and our obligation to ensure its repayment. What appears atavistic and mystifying is in fact perfectly modern, secular and democratic. The right to share and use the treasures of the past is not the privilege of the rich and powerful, nor a luxury for those who oppose them.

The idea of redemption, then, links individual liberation to that of history and society. For Benjamin, this can only occur through the destruction of wage labour in class society, an orthodox Marxist belief. But he is also, in one of the most remarkable passages in a remarkable text, able to extend that tradition, and embrace the redemption of the natural world, too. For the idea of progress, in both its capitalist and social democratic variants, has rested on the exploitation not merely of people, but also of natural resources. For Benjamin, the belief in the exploitation of nature and the junking of the radical and revolutionary dimensions of Marxism are two sides of the same coin, the profits from the exploitation of nature the inadequate compensation paid to the working class for the paucity of its social power. It was clear to Benjamin, and has become much clearer since, that such a price cannot be paid for much longer.

In one way, such an insight returns us to the classical Marxist questions of real popular control of the means of production, distribution and exchange. In another, it requires a radical rethinking not just of ideas of time and progress, but also of nature and space, to create a conception of nature as the complement of labour, not a 'resource' to be exploited. In the 'Theses' Benjamin invokes such a future in the remarkable and moving commemoration of Fourier, the nineteenth-century utopian socialist, for whom

> as a result of efficient cooperative labour, four moons would illuminate the earthly night, the ice would recede from the poles, sea water would no longer taste salty, and beasts of prey would do man's bidding. All this illustrates a kind of labour which, far from exploiting nature, is capable of delivering her of the creations which lie dormant in her womb as potentials.
>
> (Benjamin 1970: 261)

Fourier's vision (or Benjamin's vision through Fourier) stands as the reply to *The Waste Land*, which, as Maud Ellmann has pointed out in the best modern reading of the poem,[13] is full of rubbish, the polluting detritus of modern urban culture (Ellmann 1990). This beautifully prescient passage is not only remarkable in itself, but a vindication of Benjamin's method. That at a moment of mortal danger there should have flashed up this utopian vision which, with no pathos of Romantic simplicity, shows a waste land – that of industrial capitalism – redeemed, is not the smallest of Benjamin's achievements.

SUPPLEMENT

TONY DAVIES: Eliot's poem was published in 1922. Benjamin's essay was completed in 1940, though not published till 1950. You treat the two texts as to all intents and purposes contemporary, addressing the same historical predicament and conjuncture. But between 1922 (the year of *The Waste Land*) and 1940 (the year of the 'Theses') intervened some of the most cataclysmic events of world history – the emergence of Nazism and Fascism, the horrors of the Stalin regime in the USSR, the onset of the Second World War. Can you expand a bit on your reasons for not giving much weight to the historical relation, and difference, between the two texts?

JOHN BOWEN: There are differences between Eliot and Benjamin's historical positions, but not relevant ones. Their immediate situations act as catalysts of a deeper questioning of modernity. Both face the impossibility of believing in the metaphors of 'progress' and 'development', and try to think of other ways of understanding our relation to time and suffering. The links between the two texts are not historical (a 'response' to 'conditions') but conceptual and emotional. Armies of modern industrial states were creating a waste land in 1940, as they had been in 1914–18.

TD: How do you relate Eliot's later poetry and plays to *The Waste Land* and thence to Benjamin?

JB: Eliot's poetry has often been read backwards, and critics have allowed themselves to see anticipations of his later faith in *The Waste Land*'s despair. This seems to me a mistake, and to flatten the contradictions and calm the storm of Eliot's earlier and more interesting work. The *Four Quartets* is the great test of one's judgement of later Eliot. Socialists have often rejected its morality and politics, as peculiarly null in an unpleasant Uriah Heep-like way: 'The only wisdom we can hope to acquire/Is the wisdom of humility: humility is endless' ('East Coker' II; *CPP*, 179). But its questioning of time is always interesting and often, when Eliot doesn't want to turn historical process into a dull church dance, sublime.

TD: You take issue with critics who read the poem as a narrative. Does the ordering of the sections in *The Waste Land* have any rationale at all?

JB: The poem does seem weaker if reordered back-to-front or randomly, but this may be the effect of habit. The fact that *The Waste Land* has yielded up so little agreed coherence over the years is powerful evidence that its strength lies in fragments and moments. It certainly doesn't progress or tell a story, although the poem does get a little wetter as it goes along. Spatial metaphors seem more helpful than temporal ones to describe the poem, which seems to have as little sequential order as is possible without losing all hope of meaningful sequence.

TD: You briefly mention Caudwell and Spender as Benjamin's contemporaries. How useful would it be to compare the different audiences for which they wrote? And what about Eliot's criticism in the 1930s? How does it compare with what the other three were writing?

JB: It is hard to know what Benjamin's audience was in the 1930s. George Steiner says in his introduction to *The Origin of German Tragic Drama* that it was after 1931 'an extinct work'. Benjamin's autobiography, written in this period, was unpublished in his lifetime, and he found it almost impossible to find homes for his articles. The strength of English socialist writing in the 1930s was not in criticism: Spender's was even weaker than his poetry and Caudwell, in Raymond Williams's phrase, was 'not even specific enough to be wrong'. Eliot writes relatively little good criticism at this time as the productive tensions of his early work sink into the sea of faith. His most important 1930s work is in the deeply disturbed *After Strange Gods*, which Eliot refused to see republished.

TD: You mention Eliot's 'royalist conservatism', contrasting it with Benjamin's 'modernist Marxism'; but in general your reading of *The Waste Land* seems to insulate the poem quite carefully from Eliot's other writings in the surrounding years, including the essays on literary tradition in *The Sacred Wood* and the later writings on culture and national identity, many of which have a very strong pull towards precisely those 'values of coherence, order and temporal continuity' that you castigate in some of the poem's critics. This separation of the poetic and the discursive is familiar enough in New Criticism; but how does a Marxist sustain such a segregation of the text from what we know to have been the writer's own beliefs and values?

JB: I think the separation is effected by Eliot, who was able to think much more interesting and disturbed thoughts in his poetry than in his criticism. 'Tradition and the Individual Talent' has had a generally bad effect on our understanding of his verse. The essay is often seen as a fairly straightforward explication of the method of *The Waste Land*, but in fact it argues for a much more conservative aesthetic, often directly at odds with that of the poem. The later social writings are at an even greater remove.

There's a wider problem here about the constitution of a style or *œuvre* within modernist art, given that the same writer in this period often produces mature work in a very wide range of idioms. This is certainly true of Eliot. So for heuristic purposes it is better to treat *The Waste Land* as a *lusus naturae*. It is a very strange poem indeed, far too strange for the royalist, Catholic Eliot ever to feel completely happy about.

TD: The passage about Fourier from the eleventh thesis, with its image of a labour which, 'far from exploiting nature, is capable of delivering her of the creations which lie dormant in her womb', reveals how powerfully (and conventionally) gendered Benjamin's (and Marxism's) discourse is. *The Waste Land*, too, is much concerned with women and men and the (usually sordid or tragic) transactions between them. Do these texts, so radical in their historical perspectives and understandings, offer new ways of thinking about the relations between the sexes as well?

JB: One can only recognize the weakness. We shouldn't try to salvage the entire text for the kind of reading I'm making here. But I'd be loth to lose the surreal charm of Fourier's four moons.

CHAPTER 2

The Logic of Desire: The Lacanian Subject of *The Waste Land*

HARRIET DAVIDSON

[The intimacy between psychoanalysis and literature has existed from the outset. Freud, who was fond of remarking that 'the poets and artists have said it before us', drew on Sophocles' tragedy *Oedipus Tyrannus* for one of his most famous analyses of the 'family romance', the tangle of psychic pressures and identifications in which the infant personality is formed, or deformed, and wrote speculative analytic studies of Leonardo da Vinci and Dostoevsky. Early psychoanalytic criticism followed that lead, in accounts of the creative personality, understood as a special case of productively managed disorder, or in case studies that treated literary characters as actual people, like the book on *Hamlet* by Freud's Welsh friend and biographer Ernest Jones. But there was always another, arguably more fruitful way of harnessing psychoanalytic insights to the study of literary texts. In his accounts of dreams, jokes and involuntary speech mistakes, Freud himself sketched a grammar and a rhetoric of the unconscious, elucidating the symbolism – that is, the figures of representation – at work in the mediation of unconscious processes, and pointing to the mechanisms that structure their meaning, mechanisms like displacement and condensation. And early analysts were well aware of the crucial role of language in general in the operation of the therapeutic process, the 'talking cure'.

For the French psychoanalyst Jacques Lacan, the unconscious is itself 'structured like a language' (Lacan 1977: 20), its mechanisms of condensation and displacement comparable, perhaps identical, to the rhetorical figures of metonymy and metaphor. Influenced by the structuralist linguistics of Saussure, and working in conscious opposition to the humanistic and positivist 'ego psychology' of the British and North American analytic establishment, Lacan proposed an account of psychic development as a kind of text, written and rewritten not by the 'unconscious' – which is not a place, for Lacan, but a relationship, 'a sort of syntax or code' (Lacan 1977: 15) – but rather by familial and social forces beyond its control or understanding. Where they saw the individual progressing through early constraints and struggles towards full, commanding personhood (as in the popular Freudianism of films like Hitchcock's *Spellbound* and Ray's *Rebel Without a Cause*), Lacan described a process of painful and damaging accommodation to the inexorable grammar of difference, absence and loss that we call reality. In place of self-possession and successfully achieved identity, the mature adult psyche is characterized by a profound and inconsolable *lack*, a self-alienation that Lacan located, in an influential early paper, in the 'mirror stage', the process/moment in which the infant first experiences the self–other, I–you difference in which society, language, identity itself is grounded. (Here, too, a poet had 'said it before us', when Arthur Rimbaud wrote that '*Je est un autre*': I is another.) Lacan, whose own utterances, dense, allusive and punning, are closer to 'literature' than to sober scientific exposition, went on to develop a topography of psychic domains, elaborating and greatly altering Freud's theory of 'primary narcissism' and the stages of infantile sexuality: the Imaginary, a state of supposedly ideal and much-desired plenitude, unity and stasis, variously located in infancy, in sexual bliss, in a transcendent afterlife; the Symbolic, the domain of division, differentiation and lack, embodied in language, sexual difference and desire; and the Real, the ultimate ground of existence about which little can be said, since it lies outside our comprehension. Like Freud before him, Lacan has been much influenced by literary expressions of desire and its objects; and Harriet Davidson shows how readily his work lends itself to a rhetorical analysis of one of the great modern poems of lack – so readily, indeed, that as well as a Lacanian reading of *The Waste Land*, we could almost speak of an Eliotic reading of Lacan.]

TONY DAVIES

When Jacques Lacan made his definitive break with the psychoanalytic establishment of France and set up his controversial alternative school, he made a speech in Rome to a group of his followers that was scattered with references to T.S. Eliot. The 1953 'Discourse of Rome', published in English as 'The Function and Field of Speech and Language in Psychoanalysis', quotes from *The Hollow Men* in its description of alienation and alludes to the beginning and the end of *The Waste Land* by quoting the same passage from Petronius's *Satyricon* that Eliot uses to preface his poem and, in a virtual homage to *The Waste Land*, by ending with the story of the thunder from the *Upanishads*, where the thunder's DA is interpreted in three ways (Lacan 1977: 71, 77, 106). Lacan's allusions to Eliot neither justify a Lacanian reading of Eliot nor ensure its success. But the references to Eliot at this important moment in Lacan's career bring out how much Eliot spoke to Lacan's notions of desire and death, of alienation and intersubjectivity, suggesting a philosophical tie between Eliot and this poststructural thinker whose radical thought and scandalous public demeanour seem diametrically opposed to Eliot's high modernism and High Church propriety.

Modernism, even 'high' or canonical modernism, is much contested these days as critics argue about whether the initial movement of modernism and modernist form are reactionary or progressive, elitist or democratic, ahistorical or historical. There is less question about what became of modernism through the New Critical institutions which took it up, or of what Eliot himself became as editor of the *Criterion*, committed to gathering cultural authority against the unruly forces of historical change. Yet the productions called modernist retain an unresolved contradiction not entirely contained in the hierarchical dualisms implied in our critical questions.[1] Modernism is on the cusp of a change from the logical hierarchies of Enlightenment reason to a new kind of logic called in recent psychoanalysis a logic of desire, or as Lacan puts it, reason since Freud.

As a founding text of modernism, *The Waste Land* remains much battled over. For many who are critical of modernism, it is a massively repressive text whose surface fluidity and disorder only mask the rule of order and hierarchy centring the poem. More conservative critics have traditionally found comfort and delight in a similar interpretation. These conflicting positions mirror the persistent questions that have remained around *The Waste Land* since its publication in 1922: is the poem radical and new or conservative and tied to traditional values? Does the voice of a single persona dominate or does the poem challenge the coherence of any lyric voice? Is the poem about a quest and is the quest successful? Is this a religious or nihilistic poem? Does the poem represent a denial of history or an awareness of historical change? The new reader of *The Waste Land* might be particularly confused about the disparity between the seeming jumble of the poem and the many interpretations which insist that everything in the poem is really about one thing, or that all the characters are really one character.

The poem holds a deep contradiction, which solicits both kinds of responses, a contradiction similar to what is found at the heart of modernism itself between reason and the logic of desire. Early responses to the emotional texture of *The Waste Land* were often buried under the subsequent critical attention to the scholarly, the impersonal, and the mythic critique of modern society. But later in his life, Eliot protested at the way academics made *The Waste Land* into 'an important bit of social criticism'. 'To me' Eliot said, 'it was only the relief of a personal and wholly insignificant grouse against life; it is just a piece of rhythmical grumbling' (*WLF*, 1). To this disclaimer readers may respond either with relief that the poem was as meaningless as they always thought it was, or with the conviction that Eliot was up to more Old Possum tricks. But by assigning the poem to a purely personal pathology, Eliot is hardly being reductive or necessarily ingenuous. By summarily discarding the critical stance assumed to be crucial to his own theories of impersonality, objectivity and mythic order, and pointing to his own unhappiness, Eliot may help us recover the complexities and contradictions to a poem overly dominated by our image of a dour, scholastic Eliot.

Certainly the poem yearns for a kind of proper order: the elaborate trappings of the quest myth, the high culture allusions, the 'scholarly' notes, the recoil from the chaos of life, all have dominated readings of this poem. But just as certainly the poem tweaks tradition, opens itself to popular culture, and obsesses about improper behaviour, degradation and mutation. In fact the impropriety of the poem is its most evident feature: the poem not only returns again and again to improper sexual desire and its often tragic consequences, but it also questions the proper boundaries between things, indeed questions the idea of property itself. In *The Waste Land* different characters and scenes mutate confusingly into each other, while in the profuse use of allusions, the poem liberally appropriates other poets' property as its own.

These disorderly effects are not happily embraced by the poem; that will come in a more postmodern moment. But poststructural theory helps us to an interpretation that is not dominated by hierarchical dualisms which insist that *The Waste Land* sets up a hierarchy between disorder and order, between the waste land of the poem's title and a meaningful world of myth or beauty. For in the poem myth, tradition, art, even religion are subject to the same fragmentation and mutation as everything else. Nothing escapes the effects of finitude and change brought on by the stirrings of April. Recent poststructural criticism has foregrounded just this attention to absence in Eliot, not only in *The Waste Land* but also in the later religious works which some critics see as closer to a negative theology than a traditional Christianity of presence.[2] In particular, psychoanalytic theory provides a substantial way to account both for the obvious, symptomatically neurotic yearning to turn away from the movement of life to stillness, enclosure, and burial under the forgetful snow, and for the sexual and linguistic impropriety of *The Waste Land*. Curiously, given the obsessions of *The Waste Land* and Eliot's own psychic problems at the time the poem was finally composed, there is not a great deal of psychoanalytic criticism of the poem.[3] Perhaps critics are deterred by Eliot's cult of impersonality or by what I see as the inhospitality of traditionally conceived Freudian criticism, which mainly focused on thematic readings, for this poem. But Lacan's return to Freud explicitly connects linguistic and psychic mechanisms in ways that are particularly useful for literary criticism.

I would like to read *The Waste Land* through Lacan by first sketching out the groundwork of Lacan's thought and then giving a fairly close reading of the poem. Lacan presents particularly difficult problems to the critic who would use his work both because of the non-systematic nature of his system and because of his difficult style which foregrounds wordplay, allusion and non-linear argument in very modernist ways. Lacan's theoretical aversion to the whole, closed or present system is well mirrored in the fragmented way he produced his work. And yet Lacan's work is also particularly applicable to literary criticism because he makes explicit connections between linguistic and psychic mechanisms, connections which often seemed implicit but never entirely legitimate in Freud. Lacan sees his task as an interpretative one, rather than as a scientific explanatory one, thus joining the interpretative field of literary criticism.

Let me start with some conclusions, just to help guide us through Lacan's knotty thought. Lacan's three realms of the Imaginary, the Symbolic and the Real provide a helpful articulation of human experience, but provide no critical vantage point outside of systems of signification; Lacanian theory provides a new structure of subjectivity pulled between the rigidities of the Imaginary and the metonymically proliferating networks of the Symbolic which helps rethink the problem of who is speaking in *The Waste Land*; Lacan focuses attention on desire, not as a biological drive but as a condition of human finitude in which desire is both caused by and causes lack or change; Lacan explains the linguistic mechanisms of metaphor and metonymy, which alternate throughout *The Waste Land*, as psychic processes; Lacan provides a theory of waste as excess instead of emptiness. From a Lacanian perspective, *The Waste Land* is caught in a logic of desire from which there is no escape, no critical vantage point, no transcendence. In fact, the force of this logic is unending displacement. Thus the appended notes begin to seem one more displacement of desire, as do the numerous critical readings of the poem. The reader, 'hypocrite lecteur', is deliberately pulled into the chain of desire in the poem.

Lacan sees himself as returning to Freud and discovering the true innovations in the contradictions of this great modernist. Lacan's work sets out to recover Freud's most disruptive insights about the unconscious, the death drive and the ego, which have, through the course of the century, been distorted and repressed by theory such as the ego psychology that emphasizes the triumph of the ego over the id, and relegates the unconscious to the undervalued end of another dualistic hierarchy. Freud's late cultural criticism is read as massively repressive and rigid, much in the way that Eliot's cultural arguments are; both thinkers encourage this, yet also clearly have more innovative, fluid and disruptive visions at work.

Lacan's thought is commonly divided into two stages: the phenomenological and the structural, a combination at the heart of the development of poststructuralism. For structuralism provides a critique of the priority of consciousness in phenomenology, and phenomenology provides a critique of the scientistic objectivity of structuralism.[4] I would like to discuss these two stages with reference primarily to two essays: the crucial early essay 'The Mirror Stage', first written in 1936 and revised in 1949, and the 1957 essay 'The Agency of the Letter in the Unconscious or, Reason since Freud', perhaps Lacan's clearest and most complete analysis of linguistics in psychoanalysis.

In Lacan's earliest work, he refutes the lingering biologism in Freud which leads to reductive, explanatory models based on theories of instincts and drives, and looks instead to Freud's revolutionary models of interpretation of human behaviour in social terms. In spite of Lacan's insistence that he is simply returning to Freud against the later distortions of Freud's work, Lacan's work unfolds from his postulation of a new, non-Freudian psychic stage: the mirror stage. The implications of this early essay are worked out throughout Lacan's career and have revolutionary results for psychoanalysis. The mirror stage repudiates the value of the ego, Freud's most conservative notion of the self, thus definitively placing psychoanalysis within that overturning of metaphysics and rejection of Cartesian self-presence crucial to twentieth-century philosophy. 'The mirror stage', Lacan writes, sheds light 'on the formation of the I as we experience it in psychoanalysis. It is an experience that leads us to oppose any philosophy directly issuing from the Cogito' (Lacan 1977: 1). Drawing on studies from animal behaviour as well as from infant behaviour, Lacan focuses on the developmental stage when the infant recognizes itself in the mirror. This moment would seem to imply the primordial 'I' prior to complications of intersubjectivity, the ground of the self which can lead to Cartesian certainty. But for Lacan this recognition is fundamentally a misrecognition, because the totality the child sees, the integrity of the form, is opposed to the child's own sense of fragmentation and dependency that Lacan calls 'a primordial Discord' (1977: 4). The form is also external to the child, an 'other' over there in that mirror, and therefore an alienation. What the child sees in the mirror will indeed be the form for the emergence of the ego, but it is a fictional form, a 'statue in which man projects himself', a defensive, rigidified identity (1977: 2). The idea of the self as whole and unified, the Ideal self or ego-ideal, is founded upon a fundamental split and alienation. This 'specular I' is the basis for fantasies of both fragmentation and rigid totality; it is the first intimation of the split subject – the unified subject of the enounced and the fragmented subject of enunciation – which will be elaborated more fully throughout Lacan's work.

In the social world the misrecognition of the self is doubly alienated, for there the subject confuses the fictional image of the self with the images of others; thus external things are also misidentified, leading to a confusion between the 'other' which is the self and the other which is another thing (Lacan at this early stage is interested in this as a structure of paranoic alienation). Not only is the self misconceived as unitary, but also objects are similarly misconceived as fixed and rigid, thus misleading knowledge. The implications of this for Lacan are broad: the ego does not function as the normative and regulating agency that controls the impulses of the id, as it is predominately defined in Freud, but, following Freud's work on narcissism, is itself an illusory object which causes desire in our impossible yearning to be that fixed image. The total reversal here of the accepted definition of the ego is startling, as is the implication that the driving force of desire is not a biological drive or instinct, but is constituted by human insufficiency.

Lacan draws in this theory on the analysis of intersubjectivity in Hegelian phenomenology. For Hegel the consciousness of self comes initially from physical needs and the desire for objects to satisfy those needs. This self-consciousness is paradoxical: the awareness of the self is based on lack of self-sufficiency. But the lacking self receives content from the object of desire; merely physical objects may satisfy needs, but only lead to a sense of the self as physical and sufficient like a satiated animal. For humans to have true self-consciousness, human desire must be oriented not to a physical object, but towards another desiring subject. Thus the subject desires the desire of the other, maintaining the sense of lack, and also setting up the struggle for mutual recognition, the oscillations of love and hate, which lead to the destructive rigidities involved in the master–slave relationship. The master, like the mirror-stage ego, is the fiction of completion, and only wants to be looked at, desired by the other, as whole and complete; it does not want to acknowledge its own lack. The solution to the master–slave dialectic occurs, in the words of Peter Dews, 'when self-consciousness abandons its insistence upon its own autonomy and accepts its belonging to and dependence upon the human community which constitutes its substance' (Dews 1987: 58). But the self as lack must be balanced by some more positive content: 'such a community can only adequate to the aspiration toward autonomy inherent in self-consciousness when it embodies a recognition of the subjective freedom of each social member' (Dews 1987: 58). For Hegel, the solution is social and political, but while Lacan occasionally suggests a similar dependence on historical and social organizations, he tends to see the alienated ego as a universal structure of humankind, resolved in the act of speech, particularly the psychoanalytic situation.

Like Hegel, Lacan quickly leaves behind physical needs or drives to focus on desire as an intersubjective creation. Again, this is a departure from Freud, who continued to discuss drives as biological, even when, as with the death drive, he is led into contradiction. With the completion of the mirror stage, we have the simultaneous creation of desire, the unconscious, and a vague system of equivalence and mediation: 'It is this moment which decisively tips the whole of human knowledge into mediatization through the desire of the other, constitutes its objects in an abstract equivalence by the cooperation of others' (Lacan 1977: 5). Lacan is here striving to reach language as that mediating and abstracting medium which belongs to the other. But to elaborate fully the workings of this desire in creating the unconscious and in its connection to language, Lacan needs a more complex model than the mirror stage, or what he will come to call the Imaginary, can provide.

Lacan's thought develops dramatically at the end of the 1940s when he encounters structuralism in the works of anthropologist, Claude Lévi-Strauss, and the linguist, Ferdinand de Saussure, for from structuralism Lacan develops the idea of the Symbolic to place against the Imaginary and thus rewrites the drama of the emergence of the ego in slightly different terms. From Lévi-Strauss he gains a structural view of social meaning in which the subject is constructed by shifting nets of symbolic structures which carry social meaning. This idea of the subject is basically at odds with the reified ego, though many of the structures of social meaning are there to reinforce the fiction of the autonomous ego, and the ego, in turn, sees the social structures of meaning as reified in themselves: universal, unchanging and 'natural'.

The Symbolic is the 'other' that always challenges the self-sufficiency of the ego. Lacan uses the idea of the Symbolic to rewrite Freud's crucial Oedipal scene. For Lacan, the infant is able to maintain the illusion of autonomy, the image of perfect wholeness, as long as the mirror stage suggests a perfect dyad provided by the mother's absolute care. But the intervention of social realities prevents this situation of absolute care and the infant becomes aware of its insufficiency; the articulation of social structures intervenes as the law of the father or the Symbolic. Only with the recognition of the mother's absence and the feeling of insufficiency and lack does the infant internalize the absence and lack that come to haunt the ego. This recognition and internalization happen at the moment the child finds an intermediary in which it both discovers and controls this lack: language. For as in Hegelian self-consciousness, something must be absent before it becomes present, and language provides a complicated binary structure in which this dialectic takes place. This is the famous 'fort–da' stage, which Lacan seizes upon from Freud's *Beyond the Pleasure Principle*. Freud observed his grandson playing a game in which he threw a spool on a piece of thread over the side of his crib and retrieved it, saying 'fort' (gone) and 'da' (here). Freud suggests that this is how the child deals with and masters the absence of the mother. For Lacan the scene reveals the child coming to know his desire through absence and to know language through desire: 'the moment in which desire becomes human is also that in which the child is born into language' (Lacan 1977: 103). The structure of human desire as a desire of (belonging to) the other involves a dialectic of absence and presence which mediates all human interaction. The child is given the knowledge of absence and presence through the existing binary pair of signifiers 'fort' and 'da'. At this point, the structural possibilities of something not belonging to the child, that is, language or the Symbolic, become the mediation of the child's desire. This mediation creates the unconscious. Malcolm Bowie explains that in acquiring language a human 'is inserting himself into a pre-existing symbolic order and thereby submitting his desire to the systemic pressures of that order: in adopting language he allows his "free" instinctual energies to be operated upon and organized' (Bowie 1987: 109). It was Freud's great discovery to find out through the interpretation of dreams that the unconscious has a structure. Lacan extends Freud by saying that the unconscious is structured like language; the unconscious is a discourse of the Other. Lacan's unconscious is not inside, not a deep mysterious part of the self; the unconscious may be visualized as an edge between the subject and the Other that will always mediate the subject's relation to the world.[5]

Through this drama of the simultaneous creation of desire and birth into language, the child moves from the dyadic relation with the mother to a triadic relationship to society as a whole. In Freud the biological and symbolic father intervenes between the child and mother, but in Lacan the father is purely symbolic: society, language, law, the Symbolic intervenes, regulating all intersubjective relationships. Yet Lacan assumes the patriarchal law by calling the Phallus the privileged signifier of Desire. Lacan insists that the Phallus is symbolic, not biological; it represents union and wholeness. Thus the impossibility of finite, insufficient beings ever reaching unity and wholeness can be represented as a symbolic castration. Still, Lacan's continued use of these male symbols is a dilemma for many readers, because his system seems not to require this biological scene of penis envy and castration. Some feminists have embraced Lacan's work because they have sensed that Lacan equalizes the positions of male and female in the psychic drama, but the issue remains unresolved.[6] Without doubt, the symbolic in Western culture is structured towards a certain kind of male–female relation where the male occupies the position of the master (subject) and the female the slave (object), thus gendering the symbolic system in a certain way. Lacan's male-oriented language could be taken to be making a historical argument about Western society, but he does little to encourage this interpretation.

Lacan does not, I believe, contrary to some feminist critiques, make the symbolic a totalized system with no possibility for change from the law of the Father and the dominance of the Phallus. The Symbolic is an open-ended system, because the creation of the subject is always mediated by the unconscious which ensures a certain excessive and unpredictable interference with symbolic structures. The subject does not simply take on or fully replicate the symbolic structures which construct it. The inevitability of change, of a decentred system, remains, I believe, throughout Lacan's work. And we might speculate that if liberation does not mean the assumption of the Imaginary position of Master, but means a historically free subjectivity cognizant both of its dependence on others yet also of the possibilities of finitude, then we might speculate that the position of slave/object, already knowing its insufficiency, rather than that of master/subject, with no knowledge of that insufficiency, might move more easily into mature subjectivity, thus giving historically oppressed groups at least a psychic advantage. Yet the assumption of subjecthood is exactly what certain historical conditions prevent, and the force needed to change those historical conditions is likely simply to reverse the master–slave dialectic. Still, for Lacan, it seems that the female may attain full subjecthood through cultural change, while for Freud biology always seems a barrier to this process, as he consigns woman to a mysterious other he cannot understand.

The most complete explication of the convergence of desire, language and the unconscious in Lacan is in the essay 'The Agency ('L'Instance', which may also be translated 'insistence') of the Letter in the Unconscious, or Reason since Freud'. Here Lacan explicates the implications of Saussurean linguistics for his system and makes the startling and scandalous equation of linguistic and unconscious mechanisms. Lacan begins by explaining the binary nature of the sign for Saussure, who separated the signifier (material sound or letters) from the signified (concept), emphasizing the differential and arbitrary quality of both. Lacan is interested in the way Saussure diagrams these two parts of the sign as separated by a bar indicating their separate realms. For Lacan the realm of the concept is a problem which he illustrates with the amusing example of the signifiers 'Ladies' and 'Gentlemen' suspended over two identical doors. The question is what is the signified here. Certainly not the two doors, Lacan answers, but a whole symbolic system of public life of Western men and women 'subjected to the laws of urinary segregation' (Lacan 1977: 151). This system creates a chain of signification so unending that the signified is, finally, absent in the sense of being incomplete, not finished.

Because signification comes from whole symbolic systems, Lacan suggests that 'we are forced, then, to accept the notion of the incessant sliding of the signified under the signifier' (Lacan 1977: 154). The signifier, in contrast, is a 'localized structure', a sound or the letter of the essay's title, and 'it is in the chain of the signifier that meaning "insists"' (1977: 153). Because of the structures of language, meaning travels through chains of signifiers with little regard for the intentions of the user; structures of convention, metaphoric and metonymic chains (vertical and horizontal chains) carry significations in various directions; language speaks the subject, rather than the subject speaking language. Lacan is most interested in the metonymic function, which he calls the 'properly signifying function' (1977: 156). For the metonymic is a chain, the word-to-word contiguity which relies on the systemic symbolic structures, but whose action ensures that these structures are never whole or finished.

This excursion into Saussurean linguistics gives Lacan a way to talk about the creation of the subject and desire through language. For the insistence of meaning through the letter (or, the agency of the letter) is the movement of desire in the unconscious of the subject. In particular, the metonymic movement from thing to contiguous thing, from part to part searching for a non-existent whole, is the movement of desire from object to object in the search for something to fill the lack of finitude. As Anthony Wilden explains, 'metonymy, by the displacement of the "real" object of the subject's desire onto something apparently insignificant, represents the *manque d'être* (lack of being) which is constituent of desire itself' (Wilden 1986: 242). Lacan denies that he speaks metaphorically when he says: 'For the symptom *is* a metaphor whether one likes it or not, as desire *is* a metonymy however funny people may find the idea' (Lacan 1977: 175). This, for Lacan, is Freud's great discovery in *The Interpretation of Dreams*, though Freud did not have the linguistic structures which would enable him to see that the mechanisms of condensation, distortion, displacement in the unconscious are effects of the signifier. Lacan sees that Freud's Copernican revolution is not only to split the subject for ever between conscious and unconscious realms, but also to see that the unending and inescapable logic of the signifier or logic of desire continually disperses and creates the subject in the Other. Lacan subtitles Section III of 'The Agency of the Letter' 'La lettre, l'être, et l'autre' ('The letter, being and the other'), showing how the aural logic of the signifier in French punningly brings together these seemingly separate things.

Lacan rewrites the Cartesian statement of presence, which underlies philosophies of consciousness, 'I think therefore I am', as 'I think where I am not, therefore I am where I do not think' or 'I am not wherever I am the plaything of my thought; I think of what I am where I do not think to think' (Lacan 1977: 166). Lacan insists upon the 'self's radical ex-centricity to itself' (1977: 171). But though the subject is constituted by the Symbolic, 'this other to whom I am more attached than to myself' – not a particular other but a 'third locus' (1977: 173) called the Other – Lacan does not therefore do away with the particularity of the subject. For as he outlines most thoroughly in the essay 'Subversion of the Subject and the Dialectic of Desire in the Freudian Unconscious', Lacan locates the particularity of a subject in the way meaning 'insists' (inheres, recurs) along a metonymic chain (1977: 292 ff.). Peter Dews explains that, 'since no signifier follows automatically from that which precedes it, in the very *gap* between signifiers something of the subject is revealed' (Dews 1987: 100). Lacan puts it more enigmatically: 'The signifier represents a subject for another signifier.' The chain of signification is excessive, shifting, in some sense 'needing' the subject, causing and caused by the subject. The very excessiveness of the signifier, the gathering detritus and waste so repellent to the ego's desire for order and control, allow the subject to exist as a particular and acting self.

I have emphasized Lacan's use of Hegel, as Lacan does also, but Lacan also explicitly acknowledges his debt to Heidegger both at the end of his polemical 'Discourse of Rome' and at the end of 'The Agency of the Letter'. The lack or limit that is central to Lacan's discussion is also Heideggerian finitude, the being-towards-death that offers both radical limit and unfinishedness – the possibilities that inhere in a finite being. This Heideggerian dimension to Lacan's thought helps explain Lacan's Real, the third realm which he posits along with the Imaginary and the Symbolic. Lacan does not discuss the Real much, because it is the outside of language and therefore unavailable. In this way it connects to Heidegger's ontological Being and to death itself, the finitude which the Imaginary is created to hide and which drives the mediating structures of the Symbolic in a frenzied movement of desire. Like Heidegger, Lacan values not the cessation of the desire for wholeness, presence, immortality, but the acceptance of that desire as unending, unfulfillable and definitively human.

In these terms we can understand Lacan's attraction to the story of the Sibyl in the *Satyricon*. The Sibyl of Cumae, a prophetess, is rewarded by Apollo with a wish of her choice. Wishing for immortality, she is granted as many years of life as she can hold grains of sand in her hand. But forgetting to ask for eternal youth, she ages eternally. In the quoted passage, she is found hanging in a cage of living death and when asked what she now wants, she answers: 'I yearn to die.'

The Sibyl has learned the painful lesson that it is death which inspires life. In her wish for immortality, the Sibyl succumbs to the lure of the Imaginary, the cage representing the armoured defences of the ego. But the defences become a prison; she is trapped in the enounced of the immortal I, while she withers away as an empty self, cut off from death, that primordial lack of sufficiency, which would drive life, impel love and loss, and provide the metonymic field of the Symbolic in which the human ex-sists.

When *The Waste Land* is read in Lacanian terms, the Imaginary appears in the poem's opening desire for stasis, burial, 'a little life with dried tubers'. The desire for wholeness, stillness, final answers, or a central order is evident throughout the poem; in so far as it is achieved, it is a pathology represented as a prison of horrible lifelessness – the desert waste land. In contrast, the Symbolic, in which desire travels throughout cultural systems, controls the poem in its formal fragmentation and dispersal, its metonymic narratives, its obvious cultural mapping, and its sexual scenes. The Symbolic realm is also a waste land of a different sort: a land of excessive and wasteful particulars, of unfulfilment, loss, violence and death, the finite human world. The subjectivity of the poem, like Tiresias desiring the desire of the other, sifts through the scenes of the poem as the figure of both reified ego and fluid desire. The ending seems, in these terms, a rather positive one in the rejection of the Imaginary and the resigned but deliberate acceptance of the culturally inscribed structures and metonymic fragmentation of the Symbolic: 'Shall I at least set my lands in order?' the speaker concludes plaintively and pragmatically. Yet the lines that follow are others' lines and in no traditional order, giving us the speaking self of the logic of desire.

In more traditional literary terms, the 'little life with dried tubers' and the mercilessly unchanging desert of the Imaginary contrast throughout the poem with life-giving rain and the drowning sea, the life and death of the Symbolic. But looking for metonymy provides a more revealing way of articulating the poem. The opening lyric voice, with its famous rejection of the rebirth of spring, recurs throughout the poem, speaking in highly imagistic and repetitive rhetoric which at its best creates order, but at its worst creates a sense of stasis in the verse, halting the movement of language and life. This voice is associated with the desert and with a revulsion from the degradation of modern life. Because of the clarity of its purpose, it speaks with an authority and finality that ring throughout the poem. This voice is most obvious in the opening seven lines, in the 'red rock' section (ll. 19–30), in the beginning of the Unreal City section (ll. 60–8), at the close of 'The Fire Sermon' (ll. 307–11), and then, most extensively, in the first fifty lines of 'What the Thunder Said'. Though it appears fleetingly in other places, especially throughout 'The Fire Sermon', there it quickly mutates into another voice or an allusion, losing its control and the clarity of its images.

This Imaginary mode is countered by a babel of many voices, often speaking conversationally, set in metonymically rendered narrative scenes full of movement and change. Because of their variety and mutability, these voices resist categorization. The poem gives us distinct and often vivid characters in a narrative scene, such as the

Lithuanian, Marie, the hyacinth girl, Stetson, Madame Sosostris, the nervous woman, the pub woman, Tiresias, the Thames-daughters; we also hear the non-human voices of the nightingale, the cock and the thunder and voices from literature in the many allusions in the poem. At many places in the poem the boundaries between identities are unclear as voices change or mutate unexpectedly through the logic of the signifier, as at the end of 'A Game of Chess' where the pub lady's 'Goonight' mutates into Ophelia's 'good night, sweet ladies'. The stories of these characters, stories most often of desire and failure, also confusingly mutate into each other. The blurring of boundaries and the disorderly variety of voices are what make the poem so confusing to the reader; like the characters, the reader is engulfed by the metonymic dispersion of the sea of life.

The Imaginary and the Symbolic work together throughout the poem, as the strong desire for the stasis of the Imaginary is also what drives the Symbolic systems of culture and anarchy. The interweaving of these two modes provides much of the drama of the poem and provides a way to see the relations between sections of the poem that seem unrelated by theme or metaphor. For throughout the poem, order is disrupted by the forces of desire. While the formal lesson seems to be that mutability is inevitable (especially given the enigmatic ending), the desire for order remains one of the strongest desires driving the movement in the poem.

For instance, in Part I, 'The Burial of the Dead', the life-denying voice of the armoured ego which opens the poem is repeatedly interrupted by metonymic mechanisms. The stately opening to the poem presents a desire for stasis, in its anxiety about the growth, change and sexuality symbolized by April, lilacs and spring rain. The lines stymie forward movement in their repetitive syntax and the hanging participles – 'breeding', 'mixing', and 'stirring' – suggesting repeated action:

> April is the cruellest month, breeding
> Lilacs out of the dead land, mixing
> Memory and desire, stirring
> Dull roots with spring rain.
> Winter kept us warm, covering
> Earth in forgetful snow, feeding
> A little life with dried tubers.

(WL, ll. 1–7)

Speaking in tones of prophecy and despair, this lyric voice achieves a clarity and authority notable in this confusing poem. This voice is not presented as an intersubjective one; it is not particularized in a narrative, nor does it seem to be speaking to either a character or the reader. Its images tend to be familiar cultural representations for life and death such as rain and flowers, thus seeming to control the suggestiveness of the metaphors with clear ideas, as if the vehicle is only a way to get to the tenor. This is the voice of the Imaginary, wanting to maintain clear boundaries and rules, and at its most extreme hoping to halt forward movement and stop the proliferation of possibilities in life or language.

But the ego defends only imperfectly against the disruptions of desire, since it creates desire in its splitting of the subject. So in these opening lines the anxiety about change and the forces of desire cause a metonymic displacement from the painful thought of change to a seemingly irrelevant story connected only by the continuity between winter and summer. Line 8 begins as if to continue the rhythm and tone of the preceding lines, but then the syntax suddenly mutates into a chatty and incidental narrative:

> Summer surprised us, coming over the Starnbergersee
> With a shower of rain; we stopped in the colonnade,
> And went on in sunlight, into the Hofgarten,
> And drank coffee, and talked for an hour.
>
> (*WL*, ll. 8–11)

Now the participle 'coming' does not indicate eternal action by the generic 'Summer', but an action of limited duration by a particular 'us'. The angst-ridden and imagistic world of the first lines is gone; this is a realist, fairly neutral, narrative world where people drink coffee and walk and talk, a world of particular identifiable places like the Starnbergersee, a lake near Munich, and the Hofgarten, a park and café in the same city. In many ways these lines are a relief from the charged meaningfulness of the opening. Yet most readers feel anxious confronted with this new turn in the poem; these lines are not controlled by the idea or the syntax established in the opening, and they do not mean in the same way as the opening lines. While everyone literally understands what it means to drink coffee and talk for an hour, no one has yet made these lines mean anything symbolically in the way that the opening lines do. This metonymically constructed scene and other narrative scenes throughout the poem are understandable in themselves but difficult to interpret as part of the larger and unifying scheme that the opening of the poem encourages us to look for. The particular details of these scenes, like many of the characters, do not fit into a unity of idea or structure; the coffee in the Hofgarten, Lil's teeth (l. 144), the typist's stockings (l. 227) are metonymic details from the culture of the time, and they generate a context and a chain of associations which tend to disperse clear meanings.

The next line, in German, continues the elaboration of the contextual possibilities; it is seemingly from an overheard conversation, perhaps in the Hofgarten: 'Bin gar keine Russin, stamm' aus Litauen, echt deutsch' (l. 12). This line may increase the reader's anxiety even more, especially those who do not read German. But even knowing German does not much clarify the meaning of this line for the poem ('I am not Russian at all, I come from Lithuania, pure German'). This assertion of national or ethnic purity is again a sign of the ego's desire for clarity and control, but it has a good deal of satiric bite given the recent war and Eliot's thorough dislike of Germany. The effect of the line tends to disperse meaning, voice and clarity.

At line 13 still another voice seems to speak, identified, like the German-speaker before her, as a woman's. Even more than the anonymous Lithuanian, the voice undermines expectations about the consistent ego or the universality of the lyric voice. It is no accident that so many of the characters in the poem are women and that many of the stories concern sexual desire and its failure. Women in the symbolic systems of the culture of *The Waste Land* are associated with the world of desire, fertility and generation, but in this poem desire results mostly in the violence of rape or suicide, in ennui, or in frustration. Woman is both the longed for reunion with the plenitude of the mother (the Phallic mother) and also the constant reminder of human lack in woman's association with generation, with the fluid unstructured world of liquids, smells, and the open body.

Yet in the poem this symbolic function of Woman cannot be exactly equated with the female characters. Marie seems to be neither a passive object nor a symbol. She is a desiring subject. Marie's story ignores the metaphors established in the opening lines, for here the snow is connected with both memory and desire as Marie remembers a thrilling and frightening sled ride with her cousin. The movement and desire for the other are connected to freedom in an odd syntactical twist in which the 'I' becomes 'you', emphasizing the split subject and the desire for the desire of the other: 'In the mountains, there you feel free' (l. 17). But the memory of the other calls forth the pain of unfulfilled desire; in a shift from 'you' back to 'I' and to the present tense the speaker seems alone and confined: 'I read, much of the night, and go south in the winter' (l. 18).

If the stasis of the opening cannot hold because of the mutating nature of language and memory, neither can the temporal narrative keep from moving into memories of loss and change which drive the ego into isolating defences. Throughout the poem, the narrative world Eliot gives us as an alternative to the little life with dried tubers is not a pretty one; no wonder the opening voice desires to end desire. The reader, too, is caught up in this drama in a desire for meaning.

As if in reaction to the sadness of life and the instability of verse, the opening voice returns to reassert its control over both the desire and the narrative movement. The next section, often called the red rock section (ll. 19–30), repeats the imagery of the opening, removing us from the realist narrative world back into the Imaginary where the imagery is vaguely religious, repetitive, general and horrifying. The memories of Marie may be poignantly sad, but the lack of memory and desire, the lack of possibility and particularity in this world, the Sibyl's world of hopelessness, is frightening. The containment of desire tries also to contain the metonymy which creates the world.

At the end of this passage the commanding prophetic voice which promises to show us 'fear in a handful of dust' (l. 30) is abruptly countered by a short lyric passage in German, plunging the reader once again into the confusion of a totally different scene. Perhaps few readers would feel this passage in German as a refreshing change from the red rock section, yet the reader joltingly registers change in seeing a different language, different line lengths, and (with the help of Eliot's note referring us to the great tragic story of forbidden love, *Tristan und Isolde*) a new narrative. The reader is back in a diverse world of cultural objects. Here are new possibilities which seek to cover the lack of the desert, but which baffle us, perhaps making us desire the clarity of the desert once again. In translation these lines offer even more contrast to the red rock section as they speak of a scene of fresh wind, water and desire, returning the poem to the stirrings of April. The allusion to *Tristan und Isolde* is not especially painful; it is a cultural, not a personal story, therefore a displacement from the self. Here allusion displaces the anxiety about the lack revealed in desire, even though the allusion also points up the absence of the self that allows culture to speak through us and for us. Like metonymy, allusion seems to fill in the lack in the self and emphasize it at the same time.

With the return of desire, another woman speaks, again in a conversational and non-symbolic mode:

> You gave me hyacinths first a year ago;
> 'They called me the hyacinth girl.'

(ll. 35–6)

The brief and suggestive narrative of the hyacinth girl developing metonymically from the love story of Tristan and Isolde leads to an unspecified trauma:

> – Yet when we came back, late, from the hyacinth garden,
> Your arms full, and your hair wet, I could not
> Speak, and my eyes failed, I was neither
> Living nor dead, and I knew nothing,
> Looking into the heart of light, the silence.

(WL, ll. 37–41)

Returning from a seemingly sexual assignation in the garden, the speaker is overwhelmed by a strange crisis which suggests a loss of self and world in a simultaneous ecstasy of union and unbearable bereftness of self. These lines suggest the paradoxical union of love and loss, for absolute union with the other means loss of the self, as discovery of the self means a painful separation from the other. This mirror-stage trauma represents the psychic bonding of death and desire – the unbearable state of being human.

But that moment of paralysis and silence cannot hold in this changing world; the final line of this section returns to the German of *Tristan und Isolde*, diffusing the traumatic moment into a different language and into a cultural rather than personal story. The speaker's trauma is doubled but also distanced in Tristan's story, and the dying Tristan's despair at Isolde's absence is objectified into the image of the waste and empty sea: '*Oed' und leer das Meer*' (l. 42). Rather than retreating into the armoured self, the subject lets the other speak, maintaining the tension of self and other and leading the poem and reader back out into interpretation, translation and mutation. The objective correlative becomes a psychological principle.

Because there are so many allusions in *The Waste Land* – some noted by Eliot, some obvious because of the change of language, some just distant echoes for a literary reader – allusions do not offer any stabilizing framework; rather they seem like other fragments floating around in this crowded world of the poem. Thus, readers can appreciate the poem with little knowledge of the allusions and their sources, while knowing every allusion in depth provides no infallible key for reading the poem. In general, the many allusions in the poem, often quotations in other languages, undermine the notion of authentic speaking and transparent ideas, dispersing ideas into other stories, other scenes and other languages. Allusions also blur the boundaries of the poem by revealing the subtle interplay between texts: while the works alluded to influence our reading of Eliot, Eliot also changes the way we read those previous works. Thus, past literary and religious texts become not stars to steer by, but more instances of the instability and lack of autonomy of any finite thing.

The next verse paragraph provides another striking contrast in tone and *mise en scène*. As if recoiling from trauma and silence, these lines are voluble and chatty, a comic narrative revealing the mysterious-sounding Madame Sosostris, the 'wisest woman in Europe' (l. 45) who wields the prophetic power of the Tarot cards, to be only mortal, ordinary, indeed slightly silly. The Tarot plays an interesting role in *The Waste Land*. In his note to these lines, Eliot suggests that the Tarot is a kind of key to the poem, even though he freely and maybe rather slyly admits that he is mostly unfamiliar with the Tarot cards. The Tarot, like the Sibyl, represents an attempt to bypass human limitations and predict the future, seeing recurring archetypes in the place of change and particularity. Of course, the Tarot itself is a cultural object, subject to change and decay, as Eliot seems to point out in his own uninformed use of these supposedly universal cards and in his satire of the fortune-telling business. In this comic passage Sosostris's prophecy of death by water seems only melodramatically ominous in spite of its realization in Part IV, and her fear of the present – 'One must be so careful these days' (l. 59) – satirically recalls the opening fear of spring rain. Indeed, the introduction of the card of the drowned Phoenician Sailor in line 47 inspires not dread so much as wonder. The fear of death is displaced into an allusion to Shakespeare's magical romance *The Tempest* where, once again, change and metamorphosis come from death: '(Those are pearls that were his eyes. Look!)' (l. 48). The story of real exile and magic in *The Tempest* provides a telling contrast to the bogus exoticism of Madame Sosostris, yet, paradoxically, the spirit of Shakespeare's play also validates the comedy of continuing life represented by this modern sorceress.

Madame Sosostris's narrative ends satirically as the return of ordinary metonymically rendered conversation frustrates the desire for explanatory symbols like those contained in the Tarot. But the spirit of the Tarot lives on in the section which follows, beginning 'Unreal City' (l. 60). This Baudelairean invocation, which recurs at two other points in the poem (ll. 207, 376), may comment despairingly on the previous scene, but it also provides a startling contrast between the particular realism of Madame Sosostris and the general, highly imagistic vision of London as hell that follows. Heavily dependent on Dante, these lines give us an unreal vision that many readers take in a Platonic way to be the reality of our degraded urban lives. The seeming finality of this landscape again suggests the defences of the ego wanting to fix everything in an eternal vision: 'With a dead sound on the final stroke of nine' (l. 68).

But the poem will not rest in this conclusion. Once again, the vision of Imaginary stasis is disrupted by an odd bit of narrative dialogue. The narrator breaks through the horrific generality and depression of the scene and addresses a friend by the name of Stetson, a name whose American particularity almost single-handedly removes the trance created by the preceding lines. This recognition of another is both a relief from the inhuman scene, but also disruptive. For the lines which follow wildly mix modes, placing Stetson in ancient Mylae, conversationally enquiring about the corpse planted in the garden (in an echo of the opening lines), and delivering a sinister and mocking warning that the corpse just might not be so easy to keep buried. The energy of these lines (indicated by the rare spate of exclamation marks) ends 'The Burial of the Dead' not with the stasis and enclosure so desired in the opening lines, but with disruption, a grisly rebirth, and the accusatory opening out to the reader: 'You! hypocrite lecteur! – mon semblable, – mon frère!' (l. 76). In this quotation from Baudelaire, Eliot blurs the boundaries between his voice and another's and simultaneously acknowledges the reader as part of this jumble of identities. We, too, are caught in the chain of desire which keeps us searching for final meanings in a poem that solemnly suggests these final meanings and then denies them any stability.

Throughout the poem, the tension between stasis and metonymic desire is evident. Section II, 'A Game of Chess', is often cited as a vision of the sterility of the modern world. Yet the evocation of the rules of chess and the suffocating vision of a sterile life (ll. 135–8) are countered by the novelistic animation of the scenes: the eerie sensuous movement of inanimate objects in the opening scene of the boudoir, the animation of the picture of the rape of Philomel, the nervous woman's insistent and desiring questioning, the narrator's playful transposition of Shakespeare into 'O O O O that Shakespeherian Rag', the pub lady's easy and vivid chatter. All of this animation suggests the continuation of desire under the sterility of the surface. But animation begets loss. The section is dominated by women's stories of tragedy and despair in their relationships with men; scenes of the nervous woman's loneliness and Lil's domestic burdens are buttressed by allusions to Cleopatra, Dido and Ophelia, all of whom committed suicide for love (see lines 77, 92 and 172). The story of Philomel in lines 97–103 is a paradigm of the paradoxical movement of desire. The rape of Philomel by Tereus begins a series of actions and metamorphoses that turn the violated Philomel into the free-flying nightingale whose lovely song has often been a symbol for the poet's voice. But this moment of transcendence of life has little credence in Eliot's poem. Her 'inviolable voice' is again violated by the world which renders it ' "Jug Jug" to dirty ears' (l. 103), as the chain of desire continues.

The title of Section III, 'The Fire Sermon', refers to Buddha's medita-tion on the purification of sexual burning or desire by spiritual burning. But this section is ruled by sexual desire and water, here the River Thames, described as both 'sweet' and later as sweating 'Oil and tar' (ll. 266-7). The river winds its way through London present and past carrying not only the 'testimony of summer nights' (l. 179) but also a continuously mutating panoply of scenes, mostly of spiritually empty sexual encounters in which the women are rendered mechanical (the typist's automatic hand), barren (Elizabeth, the Virgin Queen), and bereft of all desire – 'I can connect / Nothing with nothing' (ll. 301-2). But Eliot's notes to 'The Fire Sermon' ensure that we see the pattern of music in this section: Spenser's Spousal song, 'Sweet Thames run softly till I end this song', the ballad of Mrs Porter, the voice of children singing from Verlaine's *Parsifal*, the degraded song of the nightingale, the music on the gramophone, the allusion to Ariel's song in *The Tempest*, the mandolin, the song of the Rhine-daughters from Wagner's *Ring*, and Eliot's songs of the Thames-daughters. The insistence of this music and its connection with sexuality in most of these songs suggests that the songs represent a continuation of desire. Indeed the possibility of music seems to be created out of these often sordid scenes, as suggested by the creation of the nightingale from rape, and the telling line from *The Tempest*: 'This music crept by me on the waters' (l. 257) insisting that the water itself, the polluted Thames, or more symbolically the life-giving and drowning water, also carries music. But the narrator sees only the despair; the ending of Section III wishes to leave behind the death, despair, and degradation, but also will leave behind the music, the life, the desire and the movement. In the final plea to leave desire behind and enter the purifying fire, language itself is purified and reduced in the final four lines of repetition and gradual reduction to the single word 'burning' as again the subject retreats into the Imaginary (ll. 308-11).

But burning, both physical and spiritual, is answered in the next sec-tion by 'Death by Water'. This short and rhythmic lyric section is made up of a series of pairs ('the cry of gulls, and the deep sea swell', 'profit and loss', 'rose and fell', 'age and youth', 'Gentile or Jew', 'turn the wheel and look to windward', 'handsome and tall') whose rocking pattern suggests the sea waves or even a maternal rocking. This rather peaceful surrender of the body to the water, the currents of life and death, seems exactly the opposite of the end of 'The Fire Sermon' and a relief from its anxiety. But neither the seeming finality of burning nor of death by water is the last word in this poem.

Instead, the burning gets taken up at the beginning of 'What the Thunder Said' with 'the torchlight red on sweaty faces' (l. 322). We are back in a barren waste, an inhuman landscape where repetition suggests a pointless circularity and the Imaginary fortress of the self is viciously defended as 'red sullen faces sneer and snarl/From doors of mudcracked houses' (ll. 344–5). In lines 347–358 the imagination tries to break out of the sterility of the desert by thinking metonymically:

> If there were water
> And no rock
> If there were rock
> And also water
> And water
> A spring
> A pool among the rock
> If there were the sound of water only
> Not the cicada
> And dry grass singing
> But sound of water over a rock
> Where the hermit-thrush sings in the pine trees
> Drip drop drip drop drop drop drop
> But there is no water

In this remarkable passage, the desire for water leads again to music as the section culminates in hearing the singing of the hermit-thrush in the pine trees. But the categorical voice of the desert stops this magical metonymic metamorphosis by insisting, 'But there is no water'. Yet this voice cannot permanently stop change. Immediately after this line, the clarity of the desert dissolves and visions begin to proliferate wildly, from the uncertain vision of the Lacanian Other, 'Who is the third who walks always beside you?' (l. 359), and the nearly inaudible reminder of the Oedipal split from the mother 'Murmur of maternal lamentation' (l. 367), to the fragmented city that 'Cracks and reforms and bursts in the violet air' (l. 372). These visions culminate in the surreal scene of a woman fiddling on her hair, bats with baby faces, and upside-down towers in a wild combination of signifiers revealing the unconscious working of desire. This whole opening to Section V has the quality of a dream, alternating between dreams of the fortress and of the fragmented body, both unconscious signifiers of the split self of the mirror stage.

But the end of the poem leaves behind that dream-like quality for a calmer, more controlled, if no less heterogeneous subjectivity. The opening up to desire is announced rather forthrightly in the crow of the cock, the flash of lightning, and the welcome gush of rain:

> Only a cock stood on the rooftree
> Co co rico co co rico
> In a flash of lightning. Then a damp gust
> Bringing rain
>
> *(WL*, ll. 391–4)

As if rewriting the formal strategy of the opening lines, here the participle 'Bringing' is attached to its object, giving a sense of release to the sexual and spiritual desire in these lines. But the seeming fulfilment is illusory; in the next lines the rain has not come and the 'limp leaves/Waited for rain' (ll. 395–6). Appropriately, the voice of thunder is neither categorical nor clear; it is a meaningless syllable, 'DA'. The poem must interpret this voice, and it does so in lines which do not clear up anything but only provide more metonymic dispersion and obscurity. The thunder is interpreted first in the Sanskrit words 'Datta', 'Dayadhvam', 'Damyata', which for most readers need to be translated into the imperatives 'give', 'sympathize', 'control'. These words are again interpreted as enigmatic lyrics in English.

Significantly, in the first lyric (ll. 401–9) the voice addresses another and the reader, placing itself in the social world:

> *Datta*: what have we given?
> My friend, blood shaking my heart
> The awful daring of a moment's surrender
> Which an age of prudence can never retract
> By this, and this only, we have existed
>
> *(WL*, ll. 401–5)

The surrender to desire *is* life, but life remains in tension with prudence and the empty rooms, just as in the following lyric (ll. 411–17) the revivifying aethereal rumours are placed in contrast with the key. In this second lyric, both the image of the prison and of the key seem to stand for the Imaginary and connect with the Sibyl's lonely cage of immortality; the desire for the key, the clear answer, the end to human

troubles, is what ironically 'confirms a prison' (l. 414).[8] Most impor-
tantly and optimistically, in the third lyric (ll. 418–22) both desire and
control are combined in the image of the sailboat both propelled by and
controlling of the wind and water. In this image the desire for order
and control is linked to the continuation of desire in the boat's movement across the water.

At the end of the poem, the desire to control desire through the ego
and the unconscious disrupting force of desire remain. In redefining 'my
lands' as a series of allusions, the subject seems to accept his desire as
the desire of the other. But that Other is not benign; the great cultural
achievements of our symbolic system are also scenarios of despair and
destruction. The variety of voices here, speaking in different languages
and different tones, indicates a world rich with possibility as well as confusion. The final words 'Shantih shantih shantih' enigmatically suggest
both a defensive quietism and more disruptive cultural dispersion.

The poem for most readers does not really end here, for the Notes
continue the quest for order, even while providing more disruptive
possibilities for interpretation. And the manuscript version of the poem,
with its extensive narrative sections, opens up even more interpretative
possibilities for the critics' desire. The strikingly heterogeneous manuscript that Eliot gathered together as he was undergoing psychological
treatment in Switzerland was submitted to the strong ego of Ezra
Pound who attempted to create a unified 'body' from the fragments:
'The thing now runs from April . . . to shantih without [a] break',
Pound asserts (Eliot 1988: 497; ellipsis in original). But a Lacanian
reading denies this ego control even while not denying the strength of
the desire to have this kind of control.

Nevertheless, the Lacanian system, like all psychoanalytic systems,
tends to be totalizing. Lacan is criticized by Derrida for this tendency
in 'Le facteur de la vérité' (1987), as he is by his generally sympathetic
readers Nancy and Lacoue-Labarthe. In their reading of 'The Agency
of the Letter' Nancy and Lacoue-Labarthe find that Lacan returns to a
centring principle, especially evident in his insistence that desire *is*
metonymy, not allowing any challenge to that ontological stability
(Nancy and Lacoue-Labarthe 1992: 101–2). In the name of structural
consistency, Lacan shuts down possibility exactly where he wishes to
open it up. In the interpretation of *The Waste Land*, this tendency is
evident in the finding of constant repetition of the same mechanisms of
metonymy and ego-fortification. While Lacan may be providing for a
certain constancy needed to have any subject at all, the interpretation
loses much of the particularity it hopes to reinstate. The other criticism

made of Lacan, particularly by leftist critics, is that these mechanisms are not historicized, and they function without regard to particular historical conditions of society (Dews 1987: 108, 234–42). The historical particularity of *The Waste Land* gets lost in the valorization of particularity itself. There is no critical vantage point in Lacan's system for seeing the clear class prejudices of *The Waste Land* nor the social or political position of the poem and the circumstances of its production in the discourses of its own day.[9] Lacanian theory returns an emotional richness to the poem, but the logic of desire may itself be a kind of tyranny.

SUPPLEMENT

TONY DAVIES: Your reading of the final section of *The Waste Land* is interestingly positive, as – and I sense a connection here – is your understanding of the Symbolic in Lacan's writing. As you know, others have found in the poem's ending a blank, autistic terminus without meaning or movement, or even a hint of 'imaginary' resolution through religion. And as for Lacan's Symbolic order, that has been seen, by some feminists especially, as a tyrannical and imprisoning system of patriarchal institutions and meanings inscribed inescapably with the Name/Law/Prohibition of the transcendental Father. In both cases we seem to be confronted with a depressing impasse, so your alternative reading is very welcome. But could you say a bit more about how you arrive at it?

HARRIET DAVIDSON: When I call the ending positive, I mean it in a relative way. Clearly neither the Imaginary nor the Symbolic is very positive in Eliot's poem, and the tone of the ending of *The Waste Land* is resigned or despairing, not affirmative. What the poem does *not* do is end in the stasis of the Imaginary; the famous ending is one of the most various and richly allusive sections of the poem. The reader is left with a feeling of incompletion and confusion, which leads one to the Notes or other sources to search for meaning. In other words, there is a sense of complex and continuing life at the end. Now, I think this quality of movement is what is crucial to the Lacanian Symbolic. Rather than being a particular system, I think we can call the Symbolic an activity. Thus while the culture we are in is oppressive, patriarchal, misogynistic, and so on these attributes are not the essence of the Symbolic but a particular manifestation of it. The Symbolic not only allows but also demands movement and change, thus allowing the possibility that things might improve or deteriorate in the future. So while this system may be intolerable, only in the acceptance of the Symbolic as a principle of activity can any particular order of the Symbolic be resisted. It is true that not everyone interprets the Symbolic in this way and feminists are particularly divided about the political implications of Lacan's work. But I do not find any indication in Lacan that the Symbolic is necessarily an oppressive system, except in the fact that we are always in a system whose terminus, for us, is death.

Eliot actually has more of a sense of life as intolerable than Lacan, because of his vision of original sin, which severely undercuts his pleasure in human life. Eliot finally turns towards God as a solution to the impasses of both the Imaginary and the Symbolic. Some might see religion itself as a turn to the Imaginary, but I think we underestimate Eliot's intelligence to say that. His religion is remarkably complex and fluid; many have noted that Eliot's theology, in its kinship to the Eastern religions he studied, resembles a dynamic and mystical negative theology more than a static theology of presence.

TD: We know that Lacan's work has been much influenced by the aesthetic and cultural discourses of modernism, and you have shown that it offers many valuable insights into modernist writing. Given the interest in psychoanalysis among intellectuals of Eliot's generation (Joyce, Lawrence and Woolf, for example), it seems surprising that psychoanalytic concepts have not been more widely used in Eliot criticism. Is that because of the political differences between the conservative Eliot and the radical Lacan, do you think?

HD: As with all interpretative frames, we are likely to find what we are look-ing for, whether we expect it or not. But certainly, Lacan is much influenced by modernism, especially philosophical modernists. Therefore, it is not sur-prising to find shared concerns between Eliot and Lacan. But modernism is large and various, and, given Eliot's resistance to psychoanalysis as part of his general resistance to the subjective, psychoanalysis has never been seen as particularly important for Eliot's work. Lacan and Eliot are not often discussed together because the current critical thinking tends to keep them apart, seeing them as temperamentally different and seeing Lacan as more radical and Eliot as more conservative than they are.

TD: To put it slightly differently: given the convergence between the con-cerns, and perhaps even the world-views, of the two writers, could we say not only that Lacan helps us to read Eliot but also that Eliot helps us to read Lacan? Can you imagine a complementary essay to your own entitled 'The Eliotic Subject of Lacan's *Ecrits*'?

HD: In spite of Lacan's resistance to systematic thinking, he nevertheless remains in Freud's hermeneutic tradition of explanation. Therefore Lacan gives us certain broad structures that are meant to explain many phenomena, while Eliot, who primarily defined himself as a poet, does not. I'm not at all sure I know what an Eliotic subject is. I can recognize Eliot's voice – which is extremely different from Lacan's voice – and I have some sense of what Eliot thought about human beings. But Eliot's writings are less consistent than Lacan's, even though Eliot's prose writings are much more accessible, mainly because Eliot was not interested in developing a system. On the other hand, reading any modernist writer helps train one for reading Lacan's cryptic text, and undoubtedly Eliot prepared me for Lacan. I would argue that the logic of desire was not invented by Lacan, but before Lacan gave us a critical language for it, readers had a hard time identifying it in Eliot and elsewhere.

CHAPTER 3

The Waste Land and the Reader's Response

STEVE ELLIS

[That a literary text only acquires meaning in the act of being read, and that readings will differ one from another, so that the meaning of the text will inevitably be to some degree provisional and circumstantial: these propositions must seem so self-evidently true to anyone under thirty that it may come as a surprise to recall how recently, and how fiercely, they were damned as heretical by the dominant modes of Anglo-American criticism. But although I.A. Richards began with an interest in the psychology of reading, and can even be claimed, now, as one of the founding figures of reader-response theory, the 'New Criticism' that developed from the writings of Richards and William Empson in England, J.C. Ransom, Cleanth Brooks and R.P. Warren in North America, is built on the categorical exclusion of the reader. For Ransom, the 'first law' of professional (that is to say, professorial) criticism is 'that it shall be objective, shall cite the nature of the object rather than its effects on the subject' (Freund 1987: 40); and this concern for the inviolable objectivity of the text was erected, by W.K. Wimsatt and M. Beardsley, into the fearsome anathema of the 'Affective Fallacy', the foolish notion that the reader has a role in determining the meaning of the text and that this is something of relevance to the literary critic. Indeed, 'meaning' itself is a suspect notion, a de-meaning, we might say, of the ontological purity of the literary object. For the New Critics, in the words of the poet Archibald MacLeish, 'a poem should not mean, but be'.

The Kantian purism of New Criticism, with its rigid separation of the ontological (the poem) from the epistemological (the reading), successfully terrorized several generations of students into supposing that their own opinions and interpretations were a vulgar irrelevance, to be suppressed in the sacramental presence of 'the words on the page'. But readers will out, and Jonathan Culler's call for the study of literature to become 'a poetics: a study of the conditions of meaning and thus a study of reading' (Culler 1980: 49) marks a decisive break with New Critical orthodoxy. In fact, Culler's own progress, from the formalism of his 1975 *Structuralist Poetics* to the reader-centred semiotics of *The Pursuit of Signs* (1981) and *On Deconstruction* (1983), can be taken as representative of the wider shift in the theoretical agenda of the 1970s. An influential figure in that shift is the German reception-theorist, Wolfgang Iser. For Iser, the literary work is not an 'object', fully present and self-sufficient in its objective existence, but an intermediate and relational term in the interaction between the text, the 'words on the page', and the reader's interpretation. The work must always be, as he puts it, 'virtual in character', not reducible either to 'the reality of the text' or to 'the subjectivity of the reader', but dynamically 'set in motion' in the interaction between the two (Iser 1978: 21). For Iser, it will be noted, the text retains an objective 'reality' of its own: reading is not Liberty Hall, and the reader's interpretative freedom is constrained by certain 'themes' and 'horizons' preordained by the formal and linguistic features of the text. In a well-known analogy, he compares it to the stars in a constellation: the stars are fixed, 'given', but the ways in which human observers join them up into a Bear, a Dog or a Lion will vary from observer to observer and from culture to culture. Iser's 'dynamic' equilibrium of textual object and reading subject has itself been attacked as a weak compromise by Stanley Fish, for whom nothing in the text is 'given', not even its own givenness (Fish 1981). For Fish, all meaning is a function of reading, and the fact that it does not collapse entirely into an anarchic open-ended solipsism in which any reading is possible is a result not of the objective 'horizon' of the textual constellation but of the pragmatic conventions and common interests of 'interpretive communities'. Some of Eliot's remarks on literary meaning suggest that he might have inclined to Fish's view; but, as Ellis points out, although the poem itself incites a riot of interpretation, the Notes to *The Waste Land* seem to reflect a desire to reimpose some thematic order. Thus the text becomes, in his account, a battleground of competing theories of reading.]

TONY DAVIES

Among the best known of the so-called 'reader response' theorists of the last two decades is Wolfgang Iser, who in *The Act of Reading* (1976; English translation 1978) outlined in considerable detail a model of the reader's 'concretization' or actualization of the literary text. Iser lays great stress on the importance of the reader as co-producer of literary meaning; meaning is not the paraphrasable content of a text but the experience the reader actually undergoes in the course of responding to textual signals. Thus the text is like a score and the reader its performer:

'literary texts initiate "performances" of meaning rather than actually formulating meanings themselves' (Iser 1978: 27). As a result 'the meaning of a literary text is not a definable entity but, if anything, a dynamic happening' (1978: 22), no longer 'an object to be defined, but . . . an effect to be experienced' (1978: 10). Iser categorizes the components that make up the textual score in *The Act of Reading*, drawing particularly on the eighteenth-century novel to exemplify that categorization.

Leaving aside the musical analogy, the text might also be seen as a set of 'instructions for meaning-production' (1978: 25), a kind of kit the reader has to assemble, or a series of signals to be decoded. But all such versions emphasize that the fruits of reading are not in the final retrieval of a 'meaning' that can stand in the place of the text itself, but in the very *act* of reading: as process, as 'dynamic happening', as a procedure constantly checking, scrutinizing and extending itself as it activates the text. The text, however, guides the reader by means of a series of features and devices that are broadly applicable to all texts; however much the 'performances' of individual readers may vary (through personal disposition and differences of historical period), the response-prompting elements within the text can be described and quantified. Thus 'a literary text contains intersubjectively verifiable instructions for meaning-production' even though 'the meaning produced may then lead to a whole variety of different experiences and hence subjective judgments' (1978: 25). Iser accepts the inevitability of different readers' responses and indeed welcomes it; there are 'many different ways in which people fulfil the reader's role set out by the text' and in many cases the 'structure of the text *allows* for different ways of fulfilment' (1978: 37, emphasis in original), though with dogmatic and didactic works the text attempts to circumscribe readerly flexibility. Even the most 'open' text has, however, its own *implied* reader, a specific readerly role offered by the text which acts as a kind of bench-mark against which individual actualizations can be compared, analysed and measured, 'a frame of reference within which individual responses to a text can be communicated to others'. The particular reader neither can nor should fulfil the implied reader's role completely but will perform a 'selective realization' of it. Nevertheless, it is precisely in the tension between the implied and real reader, in 'the role offered by the text and the real reader's own disposition' that we have the 'dynamic happening', the experience, that constitutes literary meaning (1978: 37).

What, then, are the 'instructions for meaning-production' that the literary text contains, and that the reader responds to? Iser sees texts as a composition of two major elements, which he labels the 'repertoire' and the 'strategies'; the former is thematic, the latter structural. The repertoire consists of those 'thought systems' or 'models of reality', social conventions and attitudes, philosophical and ethical ideas and so forth that exist in the text's contemporary cultural formation and that the text draws on to investigate and often challenge (or rather to make the reader investigate and challenge) (Iser 1978: 53–85). The strategies however, as the structural arrangement of the repertoire, will be the main concern of this essay and the main stimulus in the attempt to apply Iser's model to *The Waste Land*. The strategies themselves incorporate what Iser calls 'perspectives' and 'blanks'. The first are fourfold: 'generally speaking, there are four perspectives through which the pattern of the repertoire first emerges: that of the narrator, that of the characters, that of the plot, and that marked out for the reader' (1978: 96). The text is an interweaving of these perspectives, a switching backwards and forwards between them: it will come as no surprise, perhaps, that the examples Iser focuses on to substantiate his model in *The Act of Reading* are largely drawn from narrative fiction.[1] The 'blanks' are the gaps between textual segments, often marking the point at which one perspective stops and another begins; at their simplest they may occur at the end of one chapter and the beginning of another, or between the stanzas or sections of a poem. These blanks are crucial as the main incitements of readerly activity, requiring the reader to relate the segments and perspectives to one another:

> They indicate that the different segments of the text are to be connected, even though the text itself does not say so. They are the unseen joints of the text, and as they mark off schemata and textual perspectives from one another, they simultaneously trigger acts of ideation on the reader's part. Consequently, when the schemata and perspectives have been linked together, the blanks 'disappear'.
>
> (Iser 1978: 182–3)

Of course, the text may offer blanks that are more challenging and disruptive than neat chapter divisions; thus we can have 'an abrupt juxtaposition of segments . . . breaking the expected order of the text', and here 'there must automatically be a blank', representing 'not separation so much as a tacit invitation [to the reader] to find the missing link' (1978: 195–6). Indeed, the literature that prompts the most intense activity on the part of the reader will be that in which the blank-and-perspective arrangement is of this latter kind.

The perspective that the text is concentrating on at any given time Iser labels the 'theme', the other perspectives constituting at that point in the text the 'horizon', although there may not necessarily be a neat or easy division between perspectives and overlapping is often present. As the reader works through the text and finds that, when the perspective changes, the theme of one moment becomes part of the horizon of the next, she/he is involved in a constant activity of modifying conclusions hitherto reached in the light of the new theme, and of assessing the new theme against the implications of the old that now constitute the horizon. Thus the reading process becomes 'a dynamic *interaction* between text and reader' (Iser 1978: 107; emphasis in original), or 'a dynamic process of self-correction, as [the reader] formulates signifieds which he must then continually modify' (1978: 67). Initially the reader, prompted by the blank that signifies the juncture between two perspectival segments, will combine them into what Iser calls a 'referential field', which involves attending to their affinities and differences as 'reciprocal reflectors' (1978: 197). The reader then proceeds to establish a 'determinate relationship' between these segments; that is, a provisional conclusion as to what point the text is making, or which perspective is being validated, in the conjunction of these mutually modifying segments. With the introduction of the next new theme in the text the previous theme retires to the horizon, leaving, in Iser's term, a 'vacancy'; this the reader occupies with the 'determinate relationship' she/he has arrived at thus far and in the light of which the new theme is assessed (and will itself involve a reassessment of previous themes) (1978: 198). By means, then, of the text's blanks and vacancies the reader is enabled

> to combine segments into a field by reciprocal modification, to form positions from those fields, and then to adapt each position to its successor and predecessors in a process that ultimately transforms the textual perspectives, through a whole range of alternating themes and horizons, into the aesthetic object of the text.
>
> (Iser 1978: 198)

It is important to stress that the 'aesthetic object' (or, to put it simply, the 'meaning') of the text is no less than the entire *experience* of building up, weighing, modifying, rejecting and refining formulations that arise in the reading process.

Although, as remarked above, Iser mainly makes use of fiction to illustrate the structure of the literary text, he is on record as suggesting that his theories can as easily be applied to poetry.[2] *The Waste Land* might indeed be regarded as a narrative work that utilizes Iser's four perspectives in an interesting and challenging way. Certainly the following comment by Iser might seem peculiarly applicable to the type of stimulation Eliot's poem offers the reader:

> One common means of intensifying the reader's imaginative activity is suddenly to cut to new characters or even to different plot-lines, so that the reader is forced to try to find connections between the hitherto familiar story and the new, unforeseeable situations. He is faced with a whole network of possibilities, and thus begins himself to formulate missing links. The temporary withholding of information acts as a stimulus, and this is further intensified by details suggestive of possible solutions. The blanks make the reader bring the story itself to life . . .
>
> (Iser 1978: 192)

Modern literature as a whole is characterized by a greater incidence of blanks and an increase in textual 'indeterminacy' (1978: 206); indeed, the purpose of many modern works is primarily to negate traditional reading practices with a view to enabling the reader to stand outside her/his familiar experience and, via 'negativity', 'to transcend that which we are otherwise so inextricably entangled in – our own lives in the midst of the real world' (1978: 230).[3] Thus the increased 'difficulty' of modern literature always serves for Iser a positive function; being 'first and foremost a structure for eliciting responses and thereby engaging its readers' (Iser 1989: 136), it yet directs readers' attention back to the 'real world' from which the textual repertoire is taken and offers them a hitherto inaccessible position from which to criticize that world. Note that the text itself should not be viewed as making that criticism, a notion still wedded to the mimetic idea of the text reproducing reality; rather the text is seen as offering opportunities to the reader to gain for her/himself a transcendental position whereby a defamiliarized world can be questioned and, potentially, remedied.

Let us turn to *The Waste Land*, then, with its frequent blanks and sudden 'cut[s] to new characters' creating a sense of fragmentation and disorder, offset, however, by 'details suggestive of possible solutions', in Iser's phrase quoted above. Many readers of the poem will be aware of being simultaneously provided with experiences of confusion and disorientation *and* with an invitation to establish some sort of order among the textual 'fragments'. Eliot's 'Notes to The Waste Land' might be said to offer the reader in surprising detail the role of 'unifier';

this extends from the comment on line 46 on the connection that can be made between the Tarot pack figures and other personae in the poem, to the somewhat redundant instructions at lines 100, 115 and 126 to 'compare' the references to the nightingale, rats' alley and the line 'Those are pearls that were his eyes', respectively, with their occurrence elsewhere in the poem. Thus the poem might be regarded as offering the reader a 'dynamic' experience indeed, in requiring an attempt to brace together, or 'shore', a powerfully opposed sense of fragmentation. The readerly movement towards order, or unity, is not something stimulated solely by the Notes; ideas of a consistent temporal progression (compare 'the brown fog of a winter dawn' of line 61 with 'the brown fog of a winter noon' of line 208), consistent location[4] and coherent teleology (Section V features Apocalypse and a Last Judgement-type inquisition, with the London Bridge of Section I now 'falling down') are sufficiently in evidence to encourage the 'consistency-building' habits of the reader, to use a phrase from Iser (1978: 17, 18).

If we attempt to apply Iser's theme-and-horizon model to the poem in some detail we will eventually see how the text does indeed attempt to guide the reader to an apprehension of unity underlying the disorder of plural appearance. We begin with the impersonal generalization of narrator's perspective in 'April is the cruellest month . . .' which then becomes personalized with the 'us' of line 5 – introduction of protagonist or hero? or first incorporation of the reader via the universalizing pronoun, [all of] us? – and then individualized into the character's perspective with the reference to the 'I' and the naming, 'Marie', in line 15. By line 18 of the poem we are invited to see retrospectively the entire opening segment as spoken by 'Marie', though this may not cancel out the sense that the 'us' of line 5 has an application that goes beyond the members of Marie's own circle, nor that the powerful, declamatory statement of the opening four lines is being spoken by a (narratorial) voice with more authority than that we are invited to attribute to the Marie figure. In any case, in this opening segment of the poem we already feel, if we are attempting to read in Iser's terms, that the 'perspectives' of this text are merged in a provocative manner.

With the gap between lines 18 and 19 we come to the first clear 'blank' in the poem, alerting us to a change of perspective: conceivably the lines from 19 onwards might still be being spoken by Marie, though the blank and the change of tone quickly indicate that this is unlikely. The authoritative, upbraiding voice perhaps picks up something from the poem's opening; that with line 20 Eliot felt called upon to supply us with the first of the poem's specific annotations (referring us for the origin of the 'Son of man' phrase to *Ezekiel* 2:1) indicates his desire to establish the identity of the speaker of lines 19–30 (as God? or as narrator speaking with divine authority?). Thus in the opening thirty lines of the poem we have two 'segments' centring on two different perspectives and separated by a blank, which forms 'a tacit invitation . . . to find the missing link' between them (see above, p. 86). In Iser's terms the reader forms the two segments into a 'referential field' and then establishes a 'determinate relationship' between them, which s/he carries forwards as a provisional understanding of the poem thus far into the encounter with the next theme of the poem, beginning at line 31 (see above, p. 87). What that understanding might be will vary from reader to reader, but what originates it – the theme-and-horizon structure of the text – is for Iser 'intersubjectively verifiable' (see above, p. 85); that is to say, this is how the text works, however varied the results may be. The reader might feel that Marie is being castigated by the divine voice as an example of one of those (including the reader her/himself) who 'know only/A heap of broken images' (ll. 21–2); certainly the reader may want to speculate on the addressee's identity in lines 19–30, with their emphatic repetition of 'you' and 'your'. As we read the next part of the poem, however, between lines 31 and 42, we might feel that, whoever these new speakers are, and whatever the problems of relating the lines in German to the case of the hyacinth girl of line 36, and of aligning the 'I' of line 38 with previous 'I's in the poem, this part of *The Waste Land* now challenges the authority of the previous theme, in that the severe and hectoring world-view of lines 19–30 excludes the redemptive possibilities of human love ('the heart of light', l. 41).

At this point I want to stop and assure the reader that I have no intention of laboriously working through the poem perspective by perspective, as in the above sample. I simply wanted to give some idea of how the text regulates the reading process, following Iser. We may already feel in any case that *The Waste Land* will not satisfactorily repay this sort of attention: that the 'perspectives' are simply too numerous, too ambiguously connected and too difficult to categorize within Iser's four-part scheme; that, as Iser says of Joyce's *Ulysses*, 'one's first task is often simply to find out which perspective is represented by any one particular section', and that such preliminaries are as likely as not doomed to failure (Iser 1978: 102). And indeed, as I remarked above (p. 88), it is precisely the function and value of modern literature for Iser to proceed in this way, to thwart traditional reading practices and to undermine any determinate relationships the reader builds up. Through this process we are able to 'step back from our own conceptions and take a critical look at them' (1978: 194), or scrutinize our 'familiar modes of orientation' (1978: 221); in short, we realize that the demand for consistency and coherence in texts 'embodies an expectation of art which is historical in nature and consequently loses its claim to be normative' (1978: 223). That *Ulysses*, for example, does not fulfil this expectation might lead us to question not the novel, but the expectation itself; moreover, in providing us with the *experience* of the open-endedness of everyday life – 'everyday life can here be experienced as a history of ever-changing viewpoints' (1978: 210) – Joyce's novel raises the question of why traditionally literature should ever need to pattern such experience.[5]

For Iser *Ulysses* is the paradigmatic modern work; however, it will be part of my argument in what follows that *The Waste Land* is a text very unlike *Ulysses* in the role it offers to its reader, and that it does have precisely a 'central focus' which Iser argues *Ulysses* rejects (1978: 207). This leaves us for the moment with the problem of how to proceed, given that the strict application of theme-and-horizon is problematic; here we can turn for some guidance to Iser's own discussion of modern literature, with writers like Joyce and Beckett, in *The Act of Reading* and elsewhere.[6] The works of these writers thwart Iser's model, and that thwarting becomes his principal subject in an analysis that still remains centred on the reader's experience as she/he reads. I shall argue, however, that *The Waste Land* seeks to impose a more authoritarian and moralizing restriction on the reader than *Ulysses* does; rather than offering us the 'open-endedness' of everyday life it offers us the position that at bottom all life is 'one' and that that oneness is corrupt and debased.

In our brief examination of Section I of *The Waste Land* we saw some problematic merging of perspectives; for example, it was not altogether easy to establish a clear break between the character perspective of Marie and the narratorial voice in the opening section, nor was it clear that reader's and character's perspective did not merge in the sense of the addressee encompassing both the reader and the figures in the text (see above, p. 89). By the end of Section I this 'merging of perspectives' has become the text's explicit theme: the 'I' narrator who watches the crowd flow over London Bridge, who 'had not thought death had undone so many' (l. 63), addresses a colleague, Stetson – 'You who were with me . . .' (l. 70) – only to spring this identification suddenly on the reader her/himself with the concluding line, where the You-Stetson now becomes 'You! hypocrite lecteur! – mon semblable, – mon frère!'

(l. 76). Thus a triangular field of identity between narrator–character–reader is achieved as the climax of Section I; the reader is emphatically gathered into the text, becomes mirrored in the protagonists.[7] In Section II the poem sets up a strong rhetorical antithesis between 'high' and 'low' life, between Belladonna in her salon and the Cockney woman in the pub, but only to suggest that beneath the differences of discourse and social class an overriding identity (and that not a flattering one) pertains. In Section III, however, the merging of perspectives becomes paramount, enacted as it is with the introduction of the Tiresias figure, who is not only identified with the copulating couple he sees – 'And I Tiresias have foresuffered all . . .' (l. 243) – but also, as witness to the action, acts as the reader's surrogate within the text, sharing the role of spectator. Narrator, character and reader again coalesce. It hardly needs Eliot's famous note on Tiresias to indicate that the dramatis personae of the poem are indeed to be seen as one:

> Tiresias, although a mere spectator and not indeed a 'character', is yet the most important personage in the poem, uniting all the rest. Just as the one-eyed merchant, seller of currants, melts into the Phoenician Sailor, and the latter is not wholly distinct from Ferdinand Prince of Naples, so all the women are one woman, and the two sexes meet in Tiresias. What Tiresias *sees*, in fact, is the substance of the poem.
>
> (*CPP*, 78; emphasis in original)

History also is presented as 'one' in this section of the poem, the sexual depredations of modern London being seen, through the Tiresias perspective, as a historical constant, and the River Thames running through time from the Elizabeth–Leicester story to the confessions of the 'Thames-daughters' (ll. 266–306) as the recurrent setting for sexual malpractice and betrayal, implied if not stated. Religion, too, whether Eastern (Buddha) or Western (St Augustine), tells the 'one' story, of the human creature consumed by the fires of lust.

What, then, is the reader's role in all this that the text offers? I have argued above that the poem seeks to co-opt the reader into its cast of dramatis personae by merging her/his 'perspective' into those within the text; the 'experience' the text offers is then that of belonging within the waste land, of becoming another inhabitant of it, of joining the confraternity ('mon frère') of lustful and 'broken' humanity. In Iser's terms the meaning of the poem is not so much a statement, or critique, of human existence as 'waste' and infertile, as the very enactment, within the reader herself, of that understanding, of the reader's experiencing it through participation; or else the 'dynamics' that come about through the reader's resistance to this textual role. In Sections IV and V we again have the problematic conflation between specific and general addressee (the latter including the reader) that helps to co-opt the reader into the text: there are in this poem a good many references to an unnamed 'you' who seems to be part within the text, so to speak, and part outside it. Thus the body of 'Phlebas the Phoenician' in Section IV, whose death exemplifies the transience of earthly concerns and endowments – 'once handsome and tall as you' (l. 321) – is held up as a *memento mori* to a general audience of 'Gentile or Jew' (that is, everyone, reader included) which is then particularized in the following line into the internal tex-tual audience of Phlebas's fellow-voyagers, 'who turn the wheel and look to windward' (ll. 319–20) – though we should remember that the common metaphor of life as voyage implies that the 'universal' meaning is retained. Again in Section V we have the type of address – 'Who is the third who walks always beside you?' (l. 359); 'My friend, blood shaking my heart . . .' (l. 402) – where the reader may experience the sense that the lines are directed at her/him as much as at undisclosed interlocutors within the text, which once more enlists the reader among the dramatis personae and prepares for final universalizing statements like 'By this, and this only, we have existed' (l. 404) and 'We think of the key, each in his prison' (l. 413). Thus under the glare of the Last Judgement-type inquisition of Section V the reader is incriminated in the failure to 'Give, sympathise, control' – '*Datta*: what have we given?' (l. 401) – and thus turns with the final narratorial figure, Everyman/ Everywoman sitting 'upon the shore/Fishing' (ll. 423–4), to 'The peace which passeth understanding' as the only hope.

The reader of *The Waste Land* then is presented with a plurality of 'characters', voices, quotations in various languages, genres (poetry, song, nursery rhyme) and so forth, only to be brought to experience, within this abundant repertoire, the sameness of human alienation. Language and the fertility of language therefore take on in the poem the properties of a cosmetic: a way of dressing up, varying and conceal-ing this fundamentalist 'truth'. This is perhaps clearest in Section II of the poem, where those cosmetic powers can indeed be seen as the essen-tial subject: under her welter of ornament, 'strange synthetic perfumes' and descriptive excess Belladonna is as pathetic and reduced a figure as the 'antique' Lil who succeeds her. What we have here is not differentia-tion between characters but merely the rhetoric of differentiation, with a potent literary discourse, founded on Shakespeare and Pope, invest-ing Belladonna with an illusory, a purely 'cosmetic', significance. The technique is repeated in the Elizabeth and Leicester vignette in Section III (ll. 279–89), where the reference to the beauty of the barge ('A gilded shell/Red and gold') echoes the Cleopatra image that Eliot's notes on the opening of Section II refer us to: 'The barge she sat in, like a burnished throne/Burned on the water' (*Antony and Cleopatra*, II.ii.190–1). Again, language beautifies corruption, offers to conceal the burning of lust by the dazzle of descriptive glory. This position is indeed summed up and emblematized in one of the most important lines of the poem, taken from Ariel's song in *The Tempest*: 'Those are pearls that were his eyes' (I.ii.402). Here the skull itself, image of human mortality and corruption, can be metamorphosed through imaginative fantasy, through the lyricism of language, into something 'rich and strange', as Ariel's song goes on to record (I.ii.405).

When Eliot declared, after completing *The Waste Land*, that the 'water-dripping song' of Section V (ll. 331–58) constituted the only 'good' lines in the poem, he was expressing a position on poetic language that became extremely important in his later work.[8] The water-dripping song is written in a simple, repetitive, rather bare style that is appropriate to the theme it records of a literal and spiritual desert; in his later work Eliot deliberately tried to 'purge' his poetic language of its earlier luxuriance and sensuous potency in accordance with the ideas of religious purgation that became its dominant subject. Linguistic richness and decorativeness there become a kind of 'temptation' to this ascetic ideal. In *The Waste Land* we can already see adumbrated the transition that governs Eliot's whole career from the Shakespeare-inspired ornateness of Section II to the asceticism of Section V, from Ariel's song to the 'water-dripping song'; as I have remarked elsewhere, by Section V the poem has formally sloughed off the Shakespearean manner.[9]

What of the reader who refuses the poem's invitation to identify her/himself with its 'sterile' protagonists? Such a reader may well respond to those elements in the text that themselves seem to contradict its uncompromising moralizing, such as the visionary 'hyacinth garden' episode of Section I, referred to above (p. 90). Such moments of what might be inferred as ecstasy are, however, extremely uncommon in the poem; it seems likely, then, that the reader who experiences more positive, even celebratory, feelings in the course of the poem will be responding precisely to its linguistic properties, its varied poetic 'fertility'. That a poem entitled *The Waste Land* should be synonymous for many readers with an exciting efflorescence of language alerts us to a vital tension in the text bound up with its moralizing position, on the one hand, and its linguistic properties, on the other (a tension removed, incidentally, in the spare restatement of *The Waste Land*'s theme we get in *The Hollow Men*). *The Waste Land*'s wealth of varied discourse, reflected in the original heading of Sections I and II – 'He Do The Police In Different Voices' (Eliot 1971: 4–5) – might suggest to some realist-minded readers that the poem gestures to a (Dickensian) human diversity and abundance in the world that is simply too rich to be homogenized into the arid Tiresias figure – 'Old man with wrinkled female breasts' (l. 219) – and that the experience of the poem is of the many successfully *resisting* being identified as the sterile one.[10] The actual history of documented responses to the poem, however, shows little evidence of its being recuperated within a liberal-realist tradition in this way; rather what one might call the counter-moralizing readings of the poem concentrate, as remarked above, on its specifically linguistic potency. An extreme case of this might be the practice of Oxford aesthetes like Harold Acton, who 'declaimed *The Waste Land* through megaphones from balconies to bemused passers-by', where the poem seems to be being read or recited as, one might say, a pure feast of sound; certainly here any religious-moralizing or even referential element is secondary to the rhythmical and dramatic exhilaration the poem provides.[11] That Eliot himself might not have been totally unsympathetic to such a 'performance' is an important point I shall argue below, even though in his eyes a complete reading of the text (if such is possible) must attend to its didactic elements: certainly he looked askance on I.A. Richards's claim, soon after the poem was published, that *The Waste Land* effected 'a complete severance between [Eliot's] poetry and *all* beliefs'.[12] A lot of early support for the poem, then, responded to the text as an innovative and spectacular, even anarchic, composite of poetic language divorced from any moralizing function; and one also could argue that its initial reader, Ezra Pound, reshaped the text out of a similar response himself. And yet the poem, as I argued above, does have a religious-didactic programme that distinguishes it from a contemporary work like *Ulysses*, at least if we accept Iser's formulation of Joyce's novel. For Iser, *Ulysses* exemplifies modern literature in that what the reader takes from it is precisely a radical lesson in reading itself and the assumptions that go into reading; the 'implied reader' of *The Waste Land*, however, is meant to be disorientated on both an aesthetic and an ethical plane by the poem: 'You! hypocrite lecteur!'

I do not wish to imply, however, that *The Waste Land*'s implied reader (see above, p. 85) is someone who easily sees through the linguistic blandishments and riches the text offers to the moralizing emphasis that is fundamental to it, and who enrols unproblematically among the crowds that death has 'undone' (l. 63). *The Waste Land* is not a work like Bunyan's *Pilgrim's Progress* with its didactically straightforward 'counterbalancing' arrangement of perspectives, in Iser's term (Iser 1978: 100–1), and the role it offers the reader is one characterized throughout by a more profound tension and temptation; a dynamic role indeed, as noted above (p. 85). I would suggest that the implied reader of the text is one who absorbs both the text's moral programme and the shock and excitement of the language at the same time; who feels the power and exhilaration of the text, like Harold Acton and company, and yet acknowledges the moralizing mirror the protagonists hold up to her/him. This means that the experience of reading the poem would be far from easy or uncomplicated, with these two aspects of the reader's role continually coming into conflict; a constant process whereby the text seduces, chastens, excites, demoralizes, where language is indeed experienced as a temptation from the narrow way of univocal truth, and where that temptation is meant to be fully experienced, if finally overcome. What such a realization of *The Waste Land*'s implied reader's role would be like (remembering that it could only ever be a *selective* realization of it; see above, p. 85) one could only know by experiencing it for oneself; for Iser such experiences are precisely dramatic 'happenings' that resist verbal formulation: the aesthetic effect 'is in the nature of an experience and not an exercise in explanation . . . the meaning of a literary text is not a definable entity but, if anything, a dynamic happening' (Iser 1978: 22). We cannot define the 'meaning' of *The Waste Land*, then, beyond positing it in terms of the experience described above; what we can do, following Iser, is to point out those features of the text that give rise to such an experience: the merging of perspectives that is central to the poem's didactic mechanism, and the multi-voicedness that makes up its poetic power and fecundity.

Throughout his writings, Eliot shows much interest in the author–text–reader relationship, an interest that in some ways anticipates Iser's and in others throws Iser's into contrast. Eliot concentrates more than Iser on what he sees as the necessary emotional impact of the text upon the reader: though he too talks much about reading as an *experience* there is an important difference of emphasis:

> The experience of a poem is the experience both of a moment and of a lifetime. It is very much like our intenser experiences of other human beings. There is a first, or an early moment which is

unique, of shock and surprise, even of terror . . . a moment that can never be forgotten, but which is never repeated integrally; and yet which would become destitute of significance if it did not survive in a larger whole of experience, which survives inside a deeper and calmer feeling.

(SE, 250–1)

Iser's interest lies much more in reading as a cerebral and conscious process, in the formulation of coherence and consistency between textual perspectives, or in what we learn about ourselves, our world and reading when our habits of formulation are challenged. Indeed, Iser has defended himself from the charge that his theories allow no scope for basic feelings (shock, surprise, terror) that texts provoke by suggesting that the 'consistency-building' which is 'basic to text-processing' is not something we do verbally and consciously but 'is a passive synthesis occurring below the threshold of our consciousness while we read'. Thus texts will elicit reactions like frustration, shock (arguably) and laughter ('the laugh is a physical reaction to the apparent incompatibility of textual perspectives'), yet all such emotions still seem to be linked to expectations (or their rebuttal) of textual consistency, conscious or not (Iser 1989: 53–4). Here perhaps Iser's belief that his model is equally applicable to prose and poetry (see above, p. 88) might be tested, given that this belief seems to be founded solely on the idea that the division of stanzaic poetry into verses and spaces between them is a vivid illustration of segment-and-blank arrangement: 'The basic idea of theme and horizon can be strikingly illuminated by poems, where the reading of the second stanza occurs against the background or horizon of the first and is conditioned by it' (Iser 1989: 54). But this again seems to regard poems purely as narrative events, however broadly we define the term 'narrative'; the effect on the reader of rhythm, verbal arrangement, individual word-choice – the poem's micro-level, so to speak – is discounted for the sake of the macro-level, the poem's segmented blocks. What Iser's model of one stanza conditioning the next as its horizon could say of some of Eliot's own documented reading experiences – 'I was passionately fond of certain French poetry long before I could have translated two verses of it correctly' (SE, 237) – poses a problem.

Iser's model can help us analyse The Waste Land's moralizing designs on the reader, through that merging of perspectives discussed above, but it has far less to say about those responses to poetic rhythm and verbal luxuriance which constitute the reader's dangerous 'surrender' to the poem; a surrender to be experienced but not finally succumbed to. What the poem asks of its reader is a passionate and hedonistic involvement with language – the text as a kind of siren – together with the recognition and acceptance of an ethical point of view whereby these linguistic ploys of the text can be consciously grasped. To put it simply, the text demands both a rational and sensual response in equal measure, or, to borrow from his essay on 'The Metaphysical Poets', Eliot's ideal reader, like his writer, 'must look into the cerebral cortex, the nervous system, and the digestive tracts' (SE, 290). Here the function of the Notes to The Waste Land comes into play, a way perhaps of 'controlling' the excess and plural discourse that constitute the poem itself and of offering the reader at a deliberate, critical level instructions for, in Iser's phrase, 'assembling' the text: 'Tiresias, although a mere spectator and not indeed a "character", is yet the most important personage in the poem, uniting all the rest . . .' (CPP, 78). The 'shock' of the poem is a crucial element in reading, but the reader must also come to possess texts on a rational, scholarly and even ethical level, wherein, however, that shock retains something of its primary force. In his essay on Dante (1951), Eliot tackles the weighty problem of how far readers can 'appreciate' the Divine Comedy without knowing a good deal about the theological and philosophical systems that make it up, and attempts to avoid the two extremes that knowledge of the latter is essential, and that it is irrelevant to the pleasure in 'pure' poetry the Comedy can afford. He concludes:

> The enjoyment of the Divine Comedy is a continuous process. If you get nothing out of it at first, you probably never will; but if from your first deciphering of it there comes now and then some direct shock of poetic intensity, nothing but laziness can deaden the desire for fuller and fuller knowledge.
>
> (SE, 238)

And here indeed, we might think, is the ideal reading position for The Waste Land itself, one in which 'fuller and fuller knowledge' does not militate against the 'direct shock of poetic intensity' but complements it and completes it; in which the reader's position is actively serviced and deepened by the poem's Notes.

Yet here we come across one of the perennial problems in teaching a text like The Waste Land, which not only has Eliot's own Notes attached to it, but by now an extensive company of student's guides, reader's guides, master-studies and so forth. 'Genuine poetry can communicate before it is understood', Eliot says in a famous phrase

(*SE*, 238), but, as noted above, 'understanding' remains the desired end-product of poetic communication, and for this 'fuller and fuller knowledge' is necessary. Yet how far students (or anyone, for that matter) can absorb much of the information and commentary on the poem that Eliot himself inaugurated and still come through the process alive to the work's poetic 'intensity' is a question to which pedagogic experience might often provide a dispiriting answer. But the question is posed starkly by the poem and its Notes themselves: what seems to many students exciting, disruptive, anarchical, dadaist even, already starts to be clawed back by the Notes into the purlieus of the academy: 'The whole passage from Ovid is of great anthropological interest . . .' (*CPP*, 78).

Eliot himself would have been unwilling to recognize this potential fissure or antagonism between poetic intensity and scholarly interest, yet the attempts to discount it in his prose essays contemporary with *The Waste Land* (and later in the Dante essay and elsewhere) are evidence, I think, of the problem. In the famous 'Tradition and the Individual Talent' essay of 1919 he posits 'knowledge' as some mysterious essence that is not synonymous with 'a ridiculous amount of erudition' but is something that the fortunate 'absorb' while the rest have to swot up on it. To the charge that 'much learning deadens or perverts poetic sensibility' (in the writer, though the question might be raised with regard to the hypothetical reader of *The Waste Land*), he answers:

> it is not desirable to confine knowledge to whatever can be put into a useful shape for examinations . . . Some can absorb knowledge, the more tardy must sweat for it. Shakespeare acquired more essential history from Plutarch than most men could from the whole British Museum.
>
> (*SE*, 16–17)

By implication, we might say, the knowledge needed to 'understand' *The Waste Land* is not something to be sought in reams and reams of commentary but something to which there might be an (undisclosed) short-cut for the less 'tardy'. But the fullest insistence that emotional, physical and mental responses can be congruent with each other is, of course, outlined in the essay on 'The Metaphysical Poets' of 1921, in the concept of the undissociated sensibility. Modern writers (and by extension, readers) think and feel 'by fits', show a dissociation between thought and feeling: 'they do not feel their thought as immediately as the odour of a rose'. Writers from before the mid-seventeenth century, however, like John Donne, experience no incompatibility between thought and feeling but rather a subtle and complex interpenetration: 'a thought to Donne was an experience; it modified his sensibility'. Again, many of the Renaissance dramatists 'were notably erudite, and were notably men who incorporated their erudition into their sensibility: their mode of feeling was directly and freshly altered by their reading and thought'. Modern writers who are attempting to re-establish such a unification will manage to combine 'reading Spinoza' and 'the smell of cooking' into a single experience (*SE*, 286–8). And here, we might think, is a myth of reading which *The Waste Land* is founded upon, whereby the sensuous and scholarly appropriation of the poem becomes a seamless whole, and where the poem's commentary-assisted didacticism becomes as much a sensory experience as its rhythms and polyphony. But only if its 'implied reader' is John Donne. Such a notion does not contradict what was stated above (p. 96) about such an 'implied reader' finding conflict in the experience of language and its fecundity as temptress from the way of univocal truth: the poem still requires from its reader the making of ethical distinctions, even if the manner of making them calls on this unitary mode of perception.

What unites Eliot and Iser is the stress they place upon the importance of the reader in the production of literary meaning; that without readers (as professional football administrators have been known to remark of spectators) there would be no game at all. Compare Eliot's remark in *The Use of Poetry and the Use of Criticism* (the work in which he considers the 'act of reading' most fully) –

> The poem's existence is somewhere between the writer and the reader; it has a reality which is not simply the reality of what the writer is trying to 'express', or of his experience of writing it, or of the experience of the reader or of the writer as reader. Consequently the problem of what a poem 'means' is a good deal more difficult than it at first appears
>
> (*UPUC*, 30)

– with the in some ways very similar formulation in Iser:

> we may conclude that the literary work has two poles, which we might call the artistic and the aesthetic: the artistic pole is the author's text and the aesthetic is the realization accomplished by the reader. In view of this polarity, it is clear that the work itself cannot be identical with the text or with the concretization, but must be situated somewhere between the two.
>
> (Iser 1978: 21)

In this sense of the reader's elevation to partnership in the literary act, we have in both cases the legacy of I.A. Richards's work on the reading process in the 1920s; indeed, *The Use of Poetry and the Use of Criticism* is a sustained dialogue with Richards.[13] Yet nowhere does Eliot attempt to define or systematize that partnership as Iser does, nor does he have a conception that between Iser's two 'poles' there lies a unitary field where writer's and reader's input create what Iser calls the 'work'. For Iser, although the reader is free to respond to a text in her/his own way, *what* s/he responds to can always be quantified and described, originates in theme-and-horizon arrangements; the reader therefore responds 'on terms set by the text' (Iser 1980: 112). But because Eliot has no model of the textual structure acting as the controlling framework of reading, and because response for him involves a much more disruptive set of reactions – shock, surrender, terror – acting at every stage of the poem's 'micro-level' (see above, p. 97), he acknowledges a much greater degree of readerly freedom than Iser. 'What a poem means is as much what it means to others as what it means to the author', he can state quite simply (*UPUC*, 130); and, in a later essay:

> If we are moved by a poem, it has meant something, perhaps something important, to us; if we are not moved, then it is, as poetry, meaningless . . . A poem may appear to mean very different things to different readers, and all of these meanings may be different from what the author thought he meant . . . The reader's interpretation may differ from the author's and be equally valid – it may even be better. There may be much more in a poem than the author was aware of.
>
> (*OPP*, 30–1)

Iser would not necessarily dissent from these positions. But where his work is an attempt to brace all these 'meanings' together and to locate their origins within the structural features of the text, Eliot is left with a multiple series of meanings that simply *are*, and that he makes no attempt to account for, beyond suggesting that 'different interpretations *may* all be partial formulations of one thing . . . ambiguities *may* be due to the fact that the poem means more, not less, than ordinary speech can communicate' (*OPP*, 31; emphasis added). Though interpretations may be better or worse, Eliot's stress on the subjectivism of response is perhaps connected with his sense, as a writer, of the complexities of intention. Whereas for Iser texts are always purposeful acts of communication that seem very aware of their own business – 'a narrative text . . . is composed of a variety of perspectives, which outline the author's view and also provide access to what the reader is meant to visualize' (Iser 1980: 113) – for Eliot such a position begs the question that the author has in mind a 'view', or intention, or 'set of instructions' for the reader to assemble, to begin with. If Eliot himself could later confess that 'in *The Waste Land*, I wasn't even bothering whether I understood what I was saying', then it is no surprise that he might license readers to interpret the poem as they will.[14] 'The poet may hardly be aware of what he is communicating', he notes in *The Use of Poetry and the Use of Criticism* (*UPUC*, 138); it is not to be wondered at, then, that 'the problem of what a poem "means" ', which is 'a good deal more difficult than it first appears' (see above, p. 100), remains unsolved in that book.

However, if the author's interpretation of his own poem has no special status in Eliot's eyes then the implications of the comment just quoted, in which Eliot confesses to not bothering about understanding his own work, are themselves open to question. And indeed, I have argued that the poem does have purposeful designs on the reader, and that we can use Iser's term 'implied reader' to indicate that position of a moral recognition overcoming a sensual involvement with rhetoric that the poem asks us to assume. Yet such a reading position might be seen as so hazardous, so demanding in its negotiation of the tension between surrendering to, and yet mastering, rhetoric, that Eliot felt called upon to emphasize and clarify in his Notes to the poem a reading that would 'control' the plurality of discourse and make his strategy explicit. Given Eliot's difficulties in writing the poem, his awareness that 'the poet may hardly be aware of what he is communicating', the fact that Ezra Pound intervened so much in determining its final form, and finally his own undoubted sympathy with the subjectivism of readerly response, it is hardly surprising that Eliot felt the poem's moralizing designs might need some underlining. Accordingly, he outlines a focus and centre for the poem in the most traditional way, setting up Tiresias as unifying site of the poem's radical plurality ('uniting all the rest'), introducing a hierarchy of discourses ('yet the most important personage') and identifying a main 'theme' ('What Tiresias *sees*, in fact, is the substance of the poem'; and what Tiresias sees is brutish copulation). That *The Waste Land* prompted Eliot to practise the type of interpretation of his own work that normally he resolutely eschewed is some sort of testimony, perhaps, to the sheer force and disruptiveness of the poem, its need, even in its author's eyes, for some kind of control. Compare his famous response to the Oxford undergraduate who asked him what he meant by the line 'Lady, three white leopards sat under a juniper-tree' from *Ash-Wednesday*: 'I mean, "Lady, three white leopards sat under a juniper tree" . . .'.[15]

SUPPLEMENT

TONY DAVIES: You take the Notes seriously, at face value. Others have seen in them an element of possum-like mock solemnity and self-parody. Do you discount the possibility that Eliot was joking, and that readings that lean heavily on the explanatory authority of the notes may therefore be insecure?

STEVE ELLIS: It would be fairer I think to say that I take *some* of the Notes seriously, at face value. That a number of critics have seen them as an instance of 'mock solemnity and self-parody' has, of course, Eliot's own authority: in his 1956 lecture on 'The Frontiers of Criticism' he explains that the notes were only provided because of the requirements of book-length publication of the poem, 'in order to provide a few more pages of printed matter' (*OPP*, 109). They are, in a famous phrase, a 'remarkable exposition of bogus scholarship' (*OPP*, 109). But if 'what a poem means is as much what it means to others as what it means to the author' (see above, p. 101), then the same applies to a poem's commentary: its author has no monopoly of its 'meaning'. In any case, I would make a distinction between notes like that on Tiresias, which I argue has an important explanatory/controlling function, and that on, say, line 357 (*CPP*, 79): 'This is *Turdus aonalaschkae pallasii*, the hermit-thrush which I have heard in Quebec Province. Chapman says (*Handbook of Birds of Eastern North America*) . . .' and so on where Eliot is doubtless playing possum.

TD: Who, actually and empirically, is '*the* reader' of your title? J.C. Ransom says somewhere that he thought the poem unreadable until it dawned on him that it had a ready-made readership among the graduate students and young lecturers in the expanding Anglo-American universities of the 1930s. Is the readership of the poem as (perhaps depressingly) specialized and academic as that suggests?

SE: Eliot himself declared:

> the poet naturally prefers to write for as large and miscellaneous an audience as possible, and . . . it is the half-educated and ill-educated, rather than the uneducated, who stand in his way: I myself should like an audience which could neither read nor write.
>
> (*UPUC*, 152)

By this time Eliot was already thinking of the theatre as 'the ideal medium for poetry' (*UPUC*, 153), but a decade earlier, when he published *The Waste Land*, his well-known enthusiasm for the music hall might suggest his aspiration for a popular readership. I think it possible that the poem could have a degree of popular appeal; the fact that it hasn't had (which is undeniable) is more to do with the way poetry has been institutionalized in our society than with anything in the poem itself. Indeed, with a poem this challenging one might argue that all types of readers start off on a more equal footing. I wouldn't wish to exaggerate the poem's populist potential, however, and my essay argues that its implied reading combines erudition with a powerful gut response according to a pre-dissociation formula we have now lost. Eliot's crying up of Marie Lloyd may be a useful way of attacking the enervation of the intellectual classes but I don't think it seriously admits an uneducated readership to *The Waste Land*.

Within the academy there are different kinds of response, and certainly an audience primarily of 'graduate students and young lecturers' – the poem as thesis-fodder – is a depressing thought; perhaps the poem's life lies essentially in the care of a non-literary-careerist undergraduate/A-level audience (or is this my own nostalgia speaking?). Eliot was always happy to lecture to university audiences and learned societies, and would never have excluded this important component of his readership. On the other hand, there isn't much evidence that he ever canvassed his work beyond an academic/theatregoing/clerical/establishment audience.

TD: You scrupulously observe the she/he, her/him convention in talking about your reader. But, in spite of the supposed androgyny of 'Tiresias', aren't the reader identifications in the text ('mon frère', Augustine, Fisher King, Hieronymo, and so on) actually quite strongly *gendered*, with male and female figures differently positioned and observed?

SE: Yes, although I have argued that the subject of the poem is a universalist judgement that encompasses everyone, man and woman alike, I have no doubt that the poem envisages its readership as primarily male, and that where we can posit an addressee it is gendered: 'Son of man', 'hypocrite lecteur! . . . mon frère!', 'Phlebas . . . once handsome and tall as you', and so on. Since the poem resumes an overwhelmingly patriarchal literary tradition this is hardly surprising. Tiresias, 'Old man with wrinkled female breasts', is an emblem of the female as appendage to the male. That this is an attempt to control the terror of a femininity that would 'overpower' the male institution of writing, 'the priapic realm of voice', has been argued by Maud Ellman, who discusses the misogyny of a poem that is 'enthralled by the femininity that it reviles' (Ellmann 1987: 91–113).

CHAPTER 4

The Waste Land, Dialogism and Poetic Discourse

TONY PINKNEY

[What, asked the Formalists in the newly founded Soviet Union of the 1920s, is special, 'literary', about literature – not about the effect it produces but about its basic material, forms and language, and the use it puts them to? The question, as revolutionary in its implications as the infant republic in which they asked it, drove them back to a fundamental reconsideration of literary aesthetics, linguistics and stylistics. For to ask how a literary text can be distinguished from other texts (the newspaper, the scientific textbook, the political speech) requires an understanding of language in all its multifarious uses and genres, a measure of the linguistically 'normal' against which the eccentricities of the literary can be calibrated. At the same time, and quite independently, the students of an obscure Swiss linguistician called Ferdinand de Saussure were preparing for publication a course of lectures in which the elderly professor had expounded the 'arbitrary' (that is, wholly conventional and non-organic) relation between words (signifiers) and concepts (signifieds), and the source of every utterance (*parole*) in a linguistic system (*langue*) quite independent of individual language-users. A widely current pattern of depth/surface tempts to generalizing comparisons: norm/deviation and *langue/parole* look tantalizingly like the unconscious/conscious of psychoanalysis and the base/superstructure of Marxist cultural and political theory, and all, in their 'theoretical anti-humanism', threaten a similar sobering conclusion. We do not, as we fondly imagine, act/think/write; we are acted/thought/written, by forces beyond our understanding and command.

A good deal of mystery still hangs around the writings, the career, even the identity of Mikhail Bakhtin. Not that Bakhtin himself is in any doubt. A member of a group of linguists, literary critics and historians in Russia in the

1920s and early 1930s, he 'disappeared', into exile and probably into the Gulag, during the Stalin period, re-emerging in the late 1950s as a professor in an obscure university thousands of miles from Moscow. Only then did he publish the books and essays (on Rabelais, Dostoevsky, the history and theory of the novel) that he had probably written twenty or thirty years earlier; but internal evidence of the texts themselves supports the widely held theory that he was also, singly or collaboratively, the actual author of pioneering studies of linguistic and literary theory published in the names of his early friends and associates Valentin Volosinov (*Marxism and the Philosophy of Language,* 1929) and P.N. Medvedev (*The Formal Method in Literary Scholarship,* 1928). Questions of individual authorship apart (and we can take 'Bakhtin' as a *nom de plume* of the whole group), the principal contention of all these writings is to challenge the 'formalism' of the Leningrad group, of Saussurean linguistics, of Freudian psychoanalysis, and, though it could hardly be publicly admitted, of Soviet Marxist orthodoxy: the priority accorded in each case to a normative statically conceived system (the unconscious, the all-governing *langue,* the 'objective' laws of historical development) over active practice (consciousness, *parole,* collective action for change). Bakhtin is thus, certainly, one of the notable internal critics, along with Pasternak and Shostakovich, of Stalinist orthodoxy (an orthodoxy that extended, remember, even to his own specialism, in the infamous *Stalin on Linguistics,* standard text in Soviet universities). But his significance, and his influence, extend far more widely. Building on Volosinov's perception of the 'multi-accentuality' of every utterance (Volosinov 1986), the embeddedness of speech-acts not in some abstract Saussurean language system but in an active, socially differentiated process of linguistic exchange, Bakhtin developed the analysis of the interactive 'dialogism' of all language, with a heightened presence in certain literary genres, especially the modern novel. Holding the rhetorical concerns of the Formalists and the historico-social dynamics of Marxism in a mutually fruitful tension (see Bennett 1979), his work has been a fertile presence in recent literary and cultural theory. And in his study of medieval 'carnival', whose eruptions of popular misrule, although ultimately neutralized and contained by the formal hierarchies of feudal society, none the less look forward, in a profane utopianism, to the possibility of authentic critique and rupture (Bakhtin 1968), he supplied us with a concept that illuminates not only the medieval world but also, even more suggestively, the modern.]

TONY DAVIES

The actively literary linguistic consciousness at all time and everywhere . . . comes upon 'languages', and not language.

(Bakhtin 1981: 295)

Neither can anyone learn English, one can only learn a series of Englishes.

(Pound 1954: 194)

There may seem to be an air of paradox or even perversity in bringing together a powerful theoretical text on the novel as a genre and the most famous Anglo-American modernist *poem*; and this decision requires a preliminary justification – though its full vindication can only be this entire essay itself and its ability (or otherwise) to produce fruitful readings of each of its two texts in the light of the other.

Mikhail Bakhtin's seminal study of 'Discourse in the Novel', written in 1934–5 and finally appearing in English translation in 1981, runs to 160 pages and is thus virtually a book in its own right. It divides conveniently into two major sections. The first offers a largely theoretical account of the differences between 'poetic discourse' and 'novelistic discourse', though it also provides some concrete illustrations of the latter with some illuminating stylistic analysis of novels by Charles Dickens and Ivan Turgenev. The second section is a historical overview of what Bakhtin sees as the 'two stylistic lines of development of the European novel'. In this essay, I shall rely mainly on the first, more theoretical section of Bakhtin's text, though I will occasionally draw upon its later, more historical pages when these offer useful perspectives on T.S. Eliot's poetry. If we were to range across all of Bakhtin's writings rather than stick to this single (though very rich) essay, we would find many other concepts that could be brought illuminatingly to bear upon *The Waste Land*, but I shall leave these aside here and concentrate on the narrower task in hand.

A contrast between 'poetic discourse' and 'novelistic discourse' is not quite the same as a contrast between poetry and the novel as such. And in fact we shall find that, for both Bakhtin and Anglo-American modernism, the distinction between the novel and poetry is not as sharp as we might suppose. Let us look first at the distinction – or rather, its breakdown – in Bakhtin. It is, first of all, very much in the nature of the novel, as he sees it, to include poetry; the use of 'incorporated genres' is, he argues, one of its distinctive features. A second and more substantial point is that novels can be written in poetry; Pushkin's *Eugene Onegin* is the example Bakhtin most often refers to. There is thus a grey area in his work where it becomes difficult to distinguish between 'novel in verse' and 'narrative poem'. Thirdly, even some non-narrative poetry can possess a degree or even a lot of the 'dialogism' for which Bakhtin regards the novel so highly (and which I examine in detail below). Among his instances of such dialogized verse are the lyrical poetry of Jules Laforgue, who exercises such influence on T.S. Eliot's early poems, and of François Villon, who was often extolled as a poetic model by Eliot's literary mentor, Ezra Pound (and who also provides the epigraph to Eliot's own 'A Cooking Egg').

Fourthly, there is a sense for Bakhtin in which not all novels are novels. Mid-way through 'Discourse in the Novel' he takes a German critic to task for basing his theory of fiction on what Bakhtin terms 'unnovelistic novels', works which 'compositionally and thematically will be similar to a novel, will be "made" exactly as a novel is made', yet will still not *be* one (Bakhtin 1981: 327). He frequently describes how an 'authentic novel' functions, implying by his adjective that some or even many so-called novels fail to live up to their high Bakhtinian calling. Bakhtin is thus not talking about the entire empirical corpus of novels but rather a particular (though very attractive) *concept* of the novel, which not all works conventionally given that label actually match up to. So if some novels lack dialogism to the point where, for Bakhtin, they are not really novels at all, and if some poems have so much of it that they are perhaps no longer really poems after all, then the gap between the novel and poetry has narrowed considerably.

In modernist literary practice, too, there is a rapprochement between the novel and poetry in the opening decades of this century. In 'How to Read' in 1927, Ezra Pound declared: 'I believe no man can now write really good verse unless he knows Stendhal and Flaubert' (Pound 1954: 32) and the novels of Henry James, fellow-American expatriate, had a substantial impact upon both Pound and Eliot, as the title and manner of Eliot's 'Portrait of a Lady' testify. The use of the 'mask' or 'persona' in poems by Eliot, Pound and Yeats gives us, as it were, the speeches of single characters in novels with the rest of the text cut away. Their longer works may then, not too fancifully, be seen as attempts to *be* those missing novels. At any rate, Eliot's working title for *The Waste Land* – 'He Do The Police In Different Voices' – is borrowed from Dickens's *Our Mutual Friend*, which is an instance of the 'English comic novel' which has been, in Bakhtin's view, so central to the development of the novel, 'externally very vivid and at the same time historically profound' (Bakhtin 1981: 301).[1] Its epigraph – 'Nam Sibyllam quidem . . .' – is taken from Petronius's *Satyricon*, a work in which Bakhtin sees 'the germs of novelistic prose' coming together (Bakhtin 1981: 371). And in its 'Notes' *The Waste Land* famously acknowledges its indebtedness, for both 'the plan and a good deal of the incidental symbolism', to Jessie Weston's *From Ritual to Romance*

(1920), a study of those very romances which constitute, for Mikhail Bakhtin, the major medieval form of the novel.

If poetry in this period seems to be taking on characteristics of the novel, so, on the other side of the literary fence, was the novel coming closer to poetry. In many early twentieth-century novels, notoriously, precious little happens. Nineteenth-century novelistic heroes make and lose fortunes, commit adultery, get caught up in European wars and revolutions; their modernist successors, on the other hand, dip their madeleines in cups of tea (Proust), sit staring at lighthouses (Woolf), or while away the hours permutating their biscuits on the grass (Beckett). Retreating from history into the psyche, such novels offer 'poetic' rather than conventionally narrative satisfactions; in Lawrence's *The Rainbow*, say, or Woolf's *The Waves* the prose of the novel devotes itself to the cultivation of metaphor, symbol, rhythm. The British critic, F.R. Leavis, was given (largely with Lawrence in mind) to referring to the novel as a 'dramatic poem in prose', and this odd, hybrid phrase gives us a quite vivid sense of the blurring of rigid boundaries between poetry and prose fiction in the opening decades of the twentieth century.

There is, then, a certain convergence of the novel and poetry in both Bakhtinian theory and modernist writing. I have sketched this convergence of the twain in a preliminary, impressionistic way here, and we will return to it, in a fuller theoretical and historical context, towards the end of this essay. But first we must explore Bakhtin's theory of both discourse and the novel in more depth, before putting them to work in an approach to Eliot's early poetry.

I

The collection of essays in which 'Discourse in the Novel' appears in English is titled *The Dialogic Imagination*, and dialogue or dialogism or the dialogical principle is certainly the key category of Bakhtin's thought. However, he stresses throughout 'Discourse in the Novel' that dialogism has *two* senses: first, dialogue between individuals in a shared social language (its everyday sense); second, a supra-individual dialogue between social languages. In Bakhtin's view, neither of these two senses of dialogue has been taken on board in traditional thinking about language, and both have deep and radical consequences for such thinking; but of the two senses it is the second, dialogue between social languages, which most concerns him and in which he sees the uniqueness of the novel as a genre residing. It is such 'social dialogism' which will therefore govern my own approach to *The Waste Land*, but an exposition of Bakhtin must begin with the first, 'everyday' sense of dialogue.

For Bakhtin, poetry (or, better, the traditional concept of poetic discourse) is 'monological' and the novel (or novelistic discourse) is 'dialogical'; and we can begin to approach these two terms by thinking about the production of meaning in language. Take the sentence 'I am going shopping tomorrow', whose meaning seems obvious enough. But the 'meaning' we derive from it by virtue of our knowledge of English vocabulary and grammar is, for Bakhtin, not really meaning at all; it is mere 'neutral signification', not 'actual meaning' (Bakhtin 1981: 281). The latter only emerges when these five words are restored to a living, concrete context of dialogue, when they once again become a dialogical 'utterance' rather than a monological 'sentence', an inert specimen in some language textbook.

But first let us consider the sentence monologically, cut out of any living context of dialogue. 'I am going shopping tomorrow' seems, in this light, perfectly adequate to both subject and object. On the side of the subject, it satisfyingly expresses my intention; language seems to match itself precisely to what I want to say, with not a word too many or too few. On the side of the object, the sentence economically says all that needs saying about the shopping expedition, which is, so to speak, 100 per cent present in the statement. A subject in full control of his or her meanings uses a direct, unproblematical language to speak of a fully present object; God's in his heaven, and all's right with the word. Or rather, all *would* be right with the word if actual language use were ever like this idealized model, which Bakhtin terms a 'typical utopian philosopheme' of traditional linguistics and stylistics (Bakhtin 1981: 288). Actual language use, the life of 'utterances' rather than dead sentences on the linguist's microscope slide, is both messier and more invigorating than this. As we shift from neutral signification to actual meaning, to a living discursive context, our five words become a retort, a challenge, a refutation, a tactical move in a dialogical struggle:

1 '*I* am going shopping tomorrow' (i.e. *you* are not)
2 'I *am* going shopping tomorrow' (i.e. don't try to stop me, I'm determined)
3 'I am going *shopping* tomorrow' (i.e. I'm not going swimming, dancing, etc., whatever you have just suggested)
4 'I am going shopping *tomorrow*' (i.e. not today, as you want me to)

Meaning is now no longer present in the five words themselves; it resides, rather, in the relations between this utterance and what precedes and succeeds it. The utterance, that is to say, is dialogical, a retort to what has already been said and an anticipation of what is yet to come; its meaning is a function of its position in the dialogue, not locked away inside it like a kernel in a nutshell, as a monological linguistics would claim. On the side of the subject, the utterance always responds to and provokes the words of another, and on the side of the object too an 'alien word' intervenes. The shopping expedition, in actual language use, always confronts us as 'already spoken of', as shot through with the words and intentions of others:

1 the shopping-you-say-*you*-are-going-to-do
2 the shopping-you-say-I'm-not-well-enough-for
3 the shopping-that-wastes-time-you'd-rather-spend-swimming
4 the shopping-you-want-me-to-do-today

There is no 'virgin', unuttered shopping expedition that could be simply present in my own discourse. Rather, my utterance has to fight its way to the object through these competing definitions; it becomes itself precisely through its interactions with 'alien' words about that object. The traditional or monological model of language

$$\text{autonomous} \longrightarrow \text{transparent} \longrightarrow \text{virgin}$$
$$\text{subject} \qquad\qquad \text{word} \qquad\qquad \text{object}$$

gives way to a properly dialogical paradigm of language use:

$$\text{'responsive'} \longrightarrow \text{alien word} \longrightarrow \text{already-spoken-of}$$
$$\text{subject} \qquad\qquad\qquad\qquad\qquad \text{object}$$

'Dialogical', as yet, still points to a familiar, everyday sense of dialogue, involving exchanges between individuals who share a linguistic world or what Bakhtin terms an 'intra-language struggle between individual wills' (Bakhtin 1981: 273). We have not yet pressed on to the more radical meaning of dialogism as 'a struggle between socio-linguistic points of view' (1981: 273), and before we do so should turn to Bakhtin's account of the monological nature of poetic discourse. For conventional poetic discourse refuses everyday *and* social dialogism.

In a powerful paragraph of 'Discourse in the Novel', Bakhtin evokes the fate of the word in a dialogical environment:

any concrete discourse (utterance) finds the object at which it was directed already as it were overlain with qualifications, charged with value, already enveloped in an obscuring mist – or, on the contrary, by the 'light' of alien words that have already been spoken about it. It is entangled, shot through with shared thoughts, points of view, alien value judgements and accents. The word, directed towards its object, enters a dialogically agitated and tension-filled environment of alien words, value judgements and accents, weaves in and out of complex interrelationships, merges with some, recoils from others, intersects with yet a third group: and all this may crucially shape discourse, may leave a trace in all its semantic layers, may complicate its expression and influence its entire stylistic profile.

(Bakhtin 1981: 276)

Poetic discourse, however, aspires to what Bakhtin terms the 'direct word'; it conforms to the monological diagram of meaning sketched above. The direct poetic word

encounters in its orientation towards the object only the resistance of the object itself (the impossibility of its being exhausted by a word, the impossibility of saying it all), but it does not encounter . . . the fundamental and richly varied opposition of another's word. No one hinders this word, no one argues with it.

(Bakhtin 1981: 278)

These may well seem very abstract claims, but make good sense when taken into the heartlands of the British poetic tradition.

Consider the opening stanza of John Keats's 'Ode on a Grecian Urn':

Thou still uravish'd bride of quietness!
    Thou foster-child of silence and slow time,
Sylvan historian, who canst thus express
    A flowery tale more sweetly than our rhyme:
What leaf-fring'd legend haunts about thy shape
    Of deities or mortals, or of both,
        In Tempe or the dales of Arcady?
    What men or gods are these? What maidens loth?
What mad pursuit? What struggle to escape?
    What pipes and timbrels? What wild ecstasy?

Mikhail Bakhtin is a prolix writer, not usually given to memorable, pithy formulations of his central themes (hence the 160 pages of

'Discourse in the Novel'); but one such neat maxim is his claim that 'in poetry, even discourse about doubts must be cast in a discourse that cannot be doubted' (1981: 286). Keats's stanza, certainly, seems riddled by doubt: the simple antiquarian facts of the urn, let alone any deeper spiritual truths it might embody, are not at once in the poet's possession (he cannot identify the 'legend' it depicts, cannot even be sure whether the figures are gods or mortals). Moreover, and in apparent sharp contrast to Bakhtin's maxim, the very language of the poem seems afflicted by doubt about its own adequacy; it is aware that the visual imagery of the urn may be a form of narrative sweeter than its rhyme. A further dimension of doubt, implicit rather than explicit, concerns the contradictory nature of the object, the Grecian urn itself. The urn is still and silent at the beginning of the stanza, but alive with noise and movement by the end; it is virginal at the beginning, full of sexual passion – mad pursuit, wild ecstasy – by the end. Which of these two versions of the urn, the poem is already implicitly asking, is the 'true' one?

Yet all these doubts concern only the relation between the subject and object, between poet and the Grecian urn. They involve what Bakhtin terms the 'resistance of the object', the fact that it is so historically distant from Keats and therefore hard to grasp inwardly, or, at a deeper level, 'the dialectics of the object' (Bakhtin 1981: 278), the paradoxes and contradictions it contains within itself. The central paradox of 'Ode on a Grecian Urn' is that the urn, though a dead object, is more 'alive' than the living poet and his contemporaries who contemplate it, and the poem eloquently explores this contradiction through its five stanzas. But the more radical doubts which would be occasioned by the intrusion of an 'alien word' between Keats's poetic discourse and its object, by the discovery that the object (like our shopping expedition) was 'already uttered', shot through and through by the words and evaluations of others, do not occur. We seem, in the hushed, reverent intensity and intimacy ('Thou') of Keats's opening words to be witnesses of an 'eyeball-to-eyeball' encounter between poet and object, an intensely private communion between them with no interference from outside; 'the entire event', Bakhtin writes of the poetic symbol, 'is played out between the word and its object' (Bakhtin 1981: 328), and this is eminently true of Keats's poem. Yet the relation between ancient Greek art and thought and modern European culture has for centuries been a topic of intense, impassioned debate; nothing, it turns out, could be more talked about, more 'already uttered', than Keats's urn (or rather the culture from which it emerges and which it symbolizes in miniature). Yet as Bakhtin insists, poetic discourse must bring about this kind of willed linguistic amnesia:

> The word plunges into the inexhaustible wealth and contradictory multiplicity of the object itself, with its 'virginal', still 'unuttered' nature . . . It forgets that the object has its own history of contradictory acts of verbal recognition, as well as that heteroglossia that is always present in such acts of recognition.
> (Bakhtin 1981: 278)

We will come on to 'heteroglossia' in due course, since it is one of Bakhtin's central concepts. But for the moment we need only stress that (as he puts it elsewhere in 'Discourse in the Novel') in poetry every word 'that enters the work must immerse itself in Lethe, and forget its previous life in any other contexts' (Bakhtin 1981: 297). In the light of such claims, we can see that many of the terms in Keats's opening lines – still, unravish'd, quietness, silence – are not just neutral, objective descriptions of the urn, but are actively executing the project of amnesia Bakhtin is evoking; they dip the urn in Lethe, wiping out all previous alien words that have been spoken about it, all those other words that might disrupt the poet's unmediated encounter with his object.

Keats's stanza provides us with a classic instance of the monologism of traditional poetic discourse. The poet is, so to speak, fully present in his language; each word of it is directly charged with his own intentions. The language of the poem does not feel itself to be a particular poetic style, one possibility out of many with its own distinctive lexicon, tones, images, and rhythms. We, looking at it from the outside nearly two hundred years later, can certainly see it as that; its verbal density and rich sensuousness make it instantly recognizable as 'Keatsian'. But even we, as readers, must live it 'from the inside', as it would like to see itself, and then it is not just a specific style but rather the only, the inevitable language in which to meditate on these weighty issues of life and art. For both reader and poet, 'language is present to him only from inside, in the work it does to effect its intention, and not from outside, in its objective specificity and boundedness' (Bakhtin 1981: 286). And the object, even though rather more complex and contradictory than our shopping trip, is fully present in the language, too, uttered there as if for the very first time.

In the early twentieth century, too (to move much closer to T.S. Eliot), poetry still aspires to the direct monological word; but this now seems more difficult of achievement than it does in Keats. 'More often than not', Bakhtin writes, 'we experience a profound and conscious tension through which the unitary poetic language of a work rises from the heteroglot and language-diverse chaos of the literary language contemporary to it' (Bakhtin 1981: 298). This tension is particularly vivid in modernist poetics, as Bakhtin notes in one of his rare comments on contemporary literature in 'Discourse in the Novel':

> highly significant in this respect is the struggle that must be undertaken in such movements as . . . Acmeism, Dadaism, Surrealism and analogous schools with the 'qualified' nature of the object (a struggle occasioned by the idea of a return to primordial consciousness, to original consciousness, to the object itself in itself, to pure perception and so forth).
>
> (Bakhtin 1981: 277)

To Bakhtin's list of modernist isms, we should add Imagism, the movement dreamed up by Ezra Pound, Hilda Doolittle (H.D.) and Richard Aldington in a tea-shop in Kensington in the spring of 1912. Its first anthology, *Des Imagistes*, was published in March 1914, and theoretical statements by F.S. Flint, T.E. Hulme and Pound himself make it clear that the goal of Imagism is precisely the unmediated encounter with the 'object itself in itself' of which Bakhtin is speaking here. The purpose of the Image, for Hulme, is 'to arrest you, and to make you continuously see a physical thing'; poetic language is as close as we can get to 'a language of intuition which would hand over sensations bodily'. And according to Flint the aim of the Imagist poet is 'direct treatment of the "thing", whether subjective or objective'.[2]

Perhaps the most famous single Imagist poem is Ezra Pound's two-line haiku of 1911, 'In a Station of the Metro':

> The apparition of these faces in the crowd;
> Petals on a wet, black bough.

The second line certainly, in Hulmean terms, 'arrests' us and hands over a sensation bodily and unmediatedly. The heavily stressed first syllable of 'Petals' jerks us to attention, as does the sudden intrusion of this lyrical metaphor into the poem. With its three compacted heavy stresses, its alliteration and clustered consonants, 'wet black bough' seems to give us the gnarled feel of the very object it speaks about; and the poignancy of the image here is an effect of the organic delicacy and paleness of the petals set against the black, almost inorganic solidity of the bough. The direct word, plumped full with the poet's intention, renders the object vividly present; the monologism we have come to expect of poetic discourse still seems in good working order.

Yet the Image is, after all, only fifty per cent of Pound's haiku. 'Go in fear of abstractions', Pound warned the aspiring poet in his Imagist manifesto of 1913 (Jones 1972: 31), but the first half of his text is composed of precisely the kind of 'abstract', anaesthetized language he warns others against: 'The apparition of these faces in the crowd'. If we think once more of the poet's relation to his object, as we did that of Keats to his urn, it is clear that in Pound's case an 'alien word' has got there first, alien precisely in its banality and lack of any physical immediacy. The Poundian image, unlike Keatsian poetic discourse, confronts an object that is already spoken. It is therefore dialogical rather than monological; it has to confront and displace other definitions of the object, rather than parachuting directly down into the heart of a subject-matter that is being articulated for the first time. Keatsian poetic amnesia begins to lift. What impresses us most, ultimately, in the Pound haiku is the tension between two kinds of language, a clash of languages across the two lines, rather than the immediacy with which the second line delivers up its object. 'The language of the poetic genre', Bakhtin writes, 'is a unitary and singular Ptolemaic world outside of which nothing else exists and nothing else is needed' (Bakhtin 1981: 286). This is wholly true of the Keats stanza, but Pound's image *has* begun to recognize other kinds of language, even though it does so reluctantly, even tragically – and does so only to transcend them.

The clash of languages which we witness in the Pound poem is theorized by Russian Formalism, that school of literary theory which is contemporary with the Russian form of modernism (Futurism) and in polemic with which Mikhail Bakhtin develops his theory of dialogism. Formalism operates with a sharp contrast of 'ordinary' or 'practical' and 'poetic' language. The task of the poet, in a memorable phrase of Roman Jakobson, is to exercise 'organised violence upon ordinary language'. Poetic language must 'defamiliarize' or 'make strange' ordinary language, just as Pound's second line does his first line; and in the process, Formalist theory argues, it will renew experience and perceptions which have become 'automatized', or, in Viktor Shklovsky's neat phrase, 'make the stone stony'.[3] These ideas have many parallels in Imagist manifestos, and T.S. Eliot, in 'The Metaphysical Poets', uses a formulation almost as aggressive as Jakobson's own when he speaks of the poet having 'to force, to dislocate if necessary, language into his meaning' (*SE*, 289).

Bakhtin's crucial rejoinder at this point in the argument is that there is nothing ordinary about 'ordinary language'; and this takes us on to the second, more profound because *social,* sense of dialogue in his work. Though the notion is central to their poetics, Formalists had never paid much detailed attention to mere 'practical' language because they were concerned to catalogue the 'devices' (rhythm, rhyme, imagery, and so on) by which it was transmuted into poetic language. Bakhtin, on the other hand, insists that once you *do* look closely at 'ordinary language' the very category falls apart or opens up – into what he terms 'heteroglossia'. There is, in Bakhtin's view, no simple unified language that we all possess in common and which we then turn to our own individual linguistic purposes. Though there are many different ways of conceiving of such shared unitary languages – Ferdinand de Saussure's notion of *langue* is a sophisticated theoretical one, 'standard English' a more down-to-earth version – these are all false attempts to repress the extraordinary diversity of actual social language; for as Bakhtin insists, 'the actively literary linguistic consciousness at all times and everywhere . . . comes upon "languages", and not language' (Bakhtin 1981: 295). 'Heteroglossia' is formed from Greek words meaning 'different tongue', and in a vivid passage of 'Discourse in the Novel' Bakhtin evokes the processes of differentiation constantly at work in an apparently unitary national language:

> The internal stratification of any single national language into social dialects, characteristic group behaviour, professional jargons, generic languages, languages of generations and age groups, tendentious languages, languages of the authorities, of various circles and of passing fashions, languages that serve the specific sociopolitical purposes of the day, even of the hour (each day has its own slogan, its own vocabulary, its own emphases) – this internal stratification present in every language at any given moment of its historical existence is the indispensable prerequisite for the novel as a genre. The novel orchestrates all its themes . . . by means of the social diversity of speech types . . . Authorial speech, the speeches of narrators, inserted genres, the speech of characters are merely those fundamental compositional unities with whose help heteroglossia [*raznorecie*] can enter the novel.
>
> (Bakhtin 1981: 263)

We can immediately see why, for a linguistics of social heteroglossia, the novel should be the privileged literary genre. Whereas poetry strives to articulate an individual subject's vision in a language which is not open to question and which goes direct to the heart of the object, the novel (at least when it lives up to its high Bakhtinian destinies) plays off many different kinds of social language against each other; it forces them to confront each other, relativizes their claims to absolute authority, and enables the reader to feel what Bakhtin terms the 'boundedness' of each of them. Traditional stylistics, Bakhtin argues, does not know how to approach the novel; for it is in the very nature of the novel as a genre *not* to have the kind of unitary style which such a stylistics is used to analysing. Rather, he claims, 'the style of a novel is to be found in the combination of its styles; the language of a novel is the system of its "languages" ' (Bakhtin 1981: 262). These are words which are pregnant with consequences for T.S. Eliot's *The Waste Land*.

The notion of heteroglossia allows us to deepen the concept of 'dialogue' which, as we have seen, Bakhtin pits against linguistics' stress on the isolated, monological sentence. The most typical novelistic dialogue is not, he claims, a clash of individual wills in a shared social language, but rather the jarring encounter of *different* social languages, a 'struggle among socio-linguistic points of view' (Bakhtin 1981: 273). The 'distinctiveness of novelistic dialogues', he suggests, is that they 'push to the limit the mutual nonunderstanding represented by people *who speak in different languages*' (1981: 356). If, on Saturday, I say to my girlfriend 'I am going shopping tomorrow', she might prefer to go swimming instead, but we can probably sort the disagreement out within our shared secular framework. If, however, I say it to my born-again Christian grandmother and she objects that tomorrow is the sabbath, the debate can go on for a very long time without ever reconciling my secular and her fundamentalist 'socio-linguistic points of view'. Of such stuff, for Bakhtin, are authentic novelistic dialogues made.

Poetry claims to confront an unuttered object, a Grecian urn or whatever. The novel knows that its object or theme is always already uttered, spoken about – and spoken about not just by different individuals in one social language, but by different because stratified languages. This insight leads to a fine passage in which Bakhtin evokes the relation of 'prose consciousness' to its object, lines which also have an important bearing on *The Waste Land*:

> the object reveals first of all precisely the socially heteroglot multiplicity of its names, definitions and value judgements. Instead of the virginal fullness and inexhaustibility of the object itself, the prose writer confronts a multitude of routes, roads and paths laid down in the object by social consciousness . . . Along with the internal contradictions inside the object itself, the prose writer

witnesses as well the unfolding of social heteroglossia *surrounding* the object, the Tower-of-Babel mixing of languages that goes on around any object; the dialectics of the object are interwoven with the social dialogue surrounding it.

(Bakhtin 1981: 278)

The novel, Bakhtin maintains, is the 'expression of a Galilean perception of language' (1981: 366). It does not privilege any single language as having immediate access to truth or the object but is rather profoundly aware of the 'multi-languagedness' of society. The creative intentions of the novelist are accordingly not reflected directly in any one style or language, but rather are 'refracted' through many. The novelist – in a central Bakhtinian metaphor – 'orchestrates' her/his themes through a rich diversity of heteroglot styles and languages; ideally, a novel should be 'a microcosm of heteroglossia' of its own historical moment (Bakhtin 1981: 411). The technical task of the novelist is thus the creation of what Bakhtin terms an 'image of a language', the creation of a character and her/his discourse such that we sense, within the words of the individual, the *typicality* of that discourse as the language of a profession, a social class, a region, a generation, an ethnic group or whatever – as, in short, one particular language of heteroglossia striving for wider social significance in that endless, Babel-like conflict of styles and languages which is Bakhtin's invigorating vision of social life and which the novel, uniquely among literary genres, is qualified to evoke and orchestrate for its own aesthetic ends.

II

T.S. Eliot's 'Portrait of a Lady', the second poem in his 1917 volume, *Prufrock and Other Observations*, takes its title, as we have already noted, from Henry James's novel, *The Portrait of a Lady* (1881). And it should then be no surprise that Eliot's poem functions precisely as Mikhail Bakhtin claims the novel does. Unlike 'Ode on a Grecian Urn', there is no direct, unmediated authorial discourse, no 'voice of the poet'. Instead, the creative intentions of the author are 'refracted' through two competing discourses: the speeches of the lady herself and the mental responses of the young man to them. The lady's discourse resonates from its very opening words as a Bakhtinian 'image of a language':

'So intimate, this Chopin, that I think his soul
Should be resurrected only among friends

> Some two or three, who will not touch the bloom
> That is rubbed and questioned in the concert room.'
>
> *(CPP, 18)*

This is the language of the cultured, leisured upper-middle class, the language of the drawing-room or salon. It is a heteroglot dialect even more economically evoked in 'The Love Song of J. Alfred Prufrock' in the languidly ironical responses Prufrock foresees to his clamorous truth-telling:

> If one, settling a pillow by her head,
>   Should say: 'That is not what I meant at all.
>   That is not it, at all.'
>
> *(CPP, 16)*

The 'action' of 'Portrait of a Lady' is played out almost entirely on the discursive level, with the lady trying to insinuate the young man into her discourse of civilized intimacy and her interlocutor striving to remain icily outside it, to preserve his treasured 'self-possession':

> 'You let it [life] flow from you, you let it flow,
> And youth is cruel, and has no more remorse
> And smiles at situations which it cannot see.'
> I smile, of course,
> And go on drinking tea.
>
> *(CPP, 19)*

The lady throughout rhetorically presents herself as a pathos-charged figure, as 'one about to reach her journey's end' whose life has dwindled to a single, dignified gesture: 'I shall sit here, serving tea to friends' *(CPP, 20)*. She lives her language (as one would expect) wholly 'from the inside'; it is to her the inevitable, natural expression of her poignant heroism. But the young man's failure (or unwillingness) to understand her discourse – 'I smile, of course' – reduces it to an object for us; it distances and delimits it, and, indeed, takes us into what Bakhtin would regard as an archetypally novelistic situation:

> This prosaic 'estrangement' of the discourse of conventional pathos by means of an uncomprehending stupidity (simplicity, naïveté) had an enormous significance for the entire subsequent history of the novel. Even if the image of the fool . . . loses its fundamental organising role in the subsequent development of novelistic prose, nevertheless the very aspect of *not grasping* the conventions of society (the degree of society's conventionality),

not understanding lofty pathos-charged labels, things and events – such incomprehension remains almost everywhere an essential ingredient of prose style.

(Bakhtin 1981: 402)

Yet it must be admitted that this estrangement of pathos is far from complete in the poem. For the narrator is ultimately caught up *in* that pathos, enticed into the lady's discourse – as a Bakhtinian stylistics makes very clear:

> Well! and what if she should die some afternoon,
> Afternoon grey and smoky, evening yellow and rose;
> Should die and leave me sitting pen in hand . . .
>
> (*CPP*, 21)

These lines are an instance of what Bakhtin terms a 'hybrid construction', in which two distinct styles occupy a single grammatical unit. The main semantic thrust of the lines – 'what if she should die . . . and leave me' – derives from the narrator himself, yet embedded within this we recognize the very hesitations, meanderings and repetitions – 'some afternoon,/Afternoon grey and smoky, evening yellow and rose;/ Should die . . .' – which have characterized the lady's *own* language throughout the text. She does indeed, discursively speaking, 'have the advantage, after all', since her formerly self-possessed interlocutor now unknowingly ventriloquizes her 'alien' tongue.

To move to 'The Love Song of J. Alfred Prufrock' will allow us to clarify the social issues at stake in 'Portrait of a Lady'. Once again the author refracts his own intentions through competing styles: the cultivated discourse of the leisured upper-middle class,

> In the room the women come and go
> Talking of Michelangelo
>
> (*CPP*, 13)

and the language of Prufrock himself. The language of 'the women', obviously enough, is less individualized than that of the lady of 'Portrait'; even when Prufrock imagines a specific retort – 'That is not what I meant, at all' – it comes from a generic 'one' rather than an individual speaker. We are in the presence of a milieu rather than a person, a world of tea and cakes and ices, of novels, teacups and skirts that trail along the floor, the world of a generic plural – the voices, the eyes, the arms – rather than of a specific woman. And with this stronger recognition of the class nature of the women's language there comes a vivid sense of its stylistic violence:

> And I have known the eyes already, known them all –
> The eyes that fix you in a formulated phrase,
> And when I am formulated, sprawling on a pin,
> When I am pinned and wriggling on the wall,
> Then how should I begin . . . ?

> (*CPP*, 14)

Indeed, so formidable is their cultured language that Prufrock never does manage to articulate his love song after all. It remains a purely imagined discourse, while he himself, in actuality, is reduced to the speechlessness of 'a patient etherised upon a table'.

Elegant and eloquent, talking of Chopin and Michelangelo, the ladies of Eliot's early poems constitute a vivid 'image of a language'; and the particular social dialect they incarnate is, in Bakhtin's terms, 'literary language':

> everywhere and always 'literary language' has as its area of activity the conversational language of a literarily educated circle . . . The concept 'general literariness' regulates the area of spoken and written heteroglossia that swirls in from all sides on the fixed and strict poetic genre . . . 'General literariness' attempts to introduce order into this heteroglossia, to make a single, particular style canonical for it.

> (Bakhtin 1981: 381–2)

It is this 'regulative' function, whereby literary language tries to police polite discourse, that Prufrock experiences as the violence of 'formulated phrases' in the poem. Languorous these ladies may be, but they operate an impressive programme of linguistic purification, ruling Prufrock's would-be prophetic claims out of court by wearily brushing aside whatever he does utter ('That is not it . . .') or, better, by 'formulating' him linguistically and socially in their rituals of 'tea and cakes and ices' to the point where he can never articulate anything of his own in the first place.

For Prufrock certainly represents a principle of social heteroglossia, an awareness of the clamorous diversity of socially stratified languages, that aspires to break into the enclosed monological world of educated literary language. This clash between monologism and heteroglossia is imaged spatially, in that contrast between 'rooms' and 'streets' which permeates Eliot's early poetry. In 'Portrait of a Lady', the claustrophobia of a 'darkened room' and its 'atmosphere of Juliet's tomb' is contrasted to the public, open-air pleasures of admiring the monuments or reading the comics any morning in the park. In 'Prufrock' the room in which you measure out your life with coffee spoons is juxtaposed to that journey through the city streets, with the fog sensuously rubbing its back against the window panes, which Prufrock undertakes (at least in imagination, perhaps in reality) in the first two pages of the poem. In those streets one encounters new social groups, new experiences and heteroglot languages, even though none of these can come to any full articulation under the crushing monologic weight of the literary language of the salon or drawing room:

> through certain half-deserted streets,
> The *muttering* retreats
> Of restless nights in one-night cheap hotels . . .
>
> Streets that follow like a tedious *argument* . . .
>
> Shall I *say*, I have gone at dusk through narrow streets
> And watched the smoke that rises from the pipes
> Of lonely men in shirt sleeves, leaning out of windows?
>
> a street-piano, mechanical and tired
> Reiterates some worn-out common song
> With the smell of hyacinths across the garden
> (*CPP*, 13, 15, 20; emphases added)

'Streets' is probably the most powerfully charged word in the whole of Eliot's early verse, and serves as a shorthand codeword for a host of diverse, common discourses. Prufrock has listened to the socially alien words of the urban streets, in some sense even represents them; and such heteroglossia has at least relativized the claims of a monological discourse on Michelangelo, not displacing it but revealing it to be simply one language, one 'verbal-ideological viewpoint', among others. 'In the novel', Bakhtin writes, 'literary language possesses an organ for perceiving the heterodox nature of its own speech' (Bakhtin 1981: 400); and this is no less true of Eliot's early poetry. There are even passages in 'Discourse in the Novel' which read oddly like miniature Eliot poems in their own right as they too work with a sharp contrast of room and streets, monologism and heteroglossia:

> More often than not, stylistics defines itself as a stylistics of 'private craftmanship' and ignores the social life of discourse outside the artist's study, discourse in the open spaces of public

squares, streets, cities and villages, of social groups, generations and epochs.

(Bakhtin 1981: 259)

III

And so to a Bakhtinian reading of *The Waste Land*. But that reading will not be an 'interpretation' in the sense we are well used to. Bakhtin almost never sets out to say what a particular text *means*; he often notes that novelists have 'themes' and 'intentions' which they orchestrate in and through their works, but he hardly ever bothers to say, in any particular case, just what he takes these intentions to be. One reason for this is the breathtaking erudition and historical range of many of his essays, which virtually never linger on any single text for long enough to offer the kind of detailed, interpretative reading we have become accustomed to from other critics. But the crucial reason is Bakhtin's aim to produce a 'stylistics of genre' (Bakhtin 1981: 260) rather than a hermeneutical (that is, interpretative) model which could then be applied to individual works. Yet as the reader will have already gathered from my exposition, Bakhtinian stylistics is not a narrow, dryly technical exercise, a mere matter of totting up whether an author prefers semi-colons to commas across her/his text. For Bakhtin boldly declares, in the very opening paragraph of 'Discourse in the Novel', that he will 'overcome the divorce between an abstract "formal" approach and an equally abstract "ideological" approach' (1981: 259), between stylistics and (in this case Marxist) interpretation. For Bakhtin's 'sociological stylistics', the social 'meaning' of a text must be deciphered through attention to its use of language, not read off from its thematic content. Such social meaning is still not what we are now familiar with as a detailed reading or interpretation. It is more like an overall characterization of the stance of the text (or genre) within the heteroglossia of its historical epoch, of whether and to what degree it welcomes or resists heteroglossia. Or we can phrase this the other way round and argue that, for Bakhtinian analysis, 'the starting point is the point of view heteroglossia takes towards literariness' (1981: 400). In the pages that follow I will sketch such a global characterization of the relations between literariness and social heteroglossia in *The Waste Land*.

One great advantage a dialogical approach to Eliot's text has over more orthodox ones is that it dissolves the notorious issue of the 'difficulty' of the poem, packed as it is with erudite literary quotations and allusions to all sorts of cultures and historical periods. For dialogism insists that, on its way to the thematic object, one's own word has to enter into all kinds of interaction with 'alien' words, that Babel-like morass of all that has been 'already uttered' about that object. Everyday discourse, in Bakhtin's view, is at least as riddled with citations as *The Waste Land*:

> at every step one meets a 'quotation' or a 'reference' to something that a particular person said, a reference to 'people say' or 'everyone says', to the words of the person one is talking with, or to one's own previous words, to a newspaper, an official decree, a document, a book and so forth.
>
> (Bakhtin 1981: 338)

'Of all the words uttered in everyday life', he argues, 'no less than half belong to someone else' (1981: 339) – a statement which the reader can test out personally and which certainly captures the spirit of Eliot's poem. It is not so much that *The Waste Land* is 'difficult' as that most past poetry is bizarre in *its* linguistic practice, in its ruthlessly monological attempt to expunge from itself all trace of the words of others. *The Waste Land*, from a Bakhtinian perspective, simply returns discourse to itself, lets it *be* itself; it gives rein, if you like, to the dialogic tendencies inherent in all language.

Let us approach the poem by considering its treatment of what seems, after 'Prufock' and 'Portrait of a Lady', the archetypal Eliot motif: the cultured, upper-class woman in her room.

> The Chair she sat in, like a burnished throne,
> Glowed on the marble, where the glass
> Held up by standards wrought with fruited vines
> From which a golden Cupidon peeped out
> (Another hid his eyes behind his wing)
> Doubled the flames of sevenbranched candelabra
> Reflecting light upon the table as
> The glitter of her jewels rose to meet it,
> From satin cases poured in rich profusion.
> In vials of ivory and coloured glass
> Unstoppered, lurked her strange synthetic perfumes,
> Unguent, powdered, or liquid – troubled, confused
> And drowned the sense in odours; stirred by the air
> That freshened from the window, these ascended
> In fattening the prolonged candle-flames,

Flung their smoke into the laquearia,
Stirring the pattern on the coffered ceiling.

(*CPP*, 64)

As the working title of *The Waste Land* suggests, Eliot is here, in good novelistic fashion, 'doing the police in different voices'. Or, to put the same point in more strictly Bakhtinian terms, we are here in the presence of 'parodic stylization', the kind of 'double-voiced' discourse characteristic of the novel. That this is a 'stylization', the creation of a socially typical image of a language, is clear from the first line on. With its lofty diction ('burnished', 'wrought', 'fruited') and equally lofty objects (marble, candelabra, laquearia), this is the language of epic ceremoniousness, of pomp and circumstance; and the literary references Eliot gives in his Notes – *Antony and Cleopatra*, Virgil's *Aeneid* and, later, *Paradise Lost* and Ovid's *Metamorphoses* – all belong appositely in this context. This is discourse of an impressive stateliness, and yet only a few lines in the reader begins to have reservations and doubts. The spatial layout of the room seems a little too hard to follow, surely; we begin to lose our way around these two long, convoluted sentences, whose rich linguistic profusion troubles, confuses and drowns *us* in a surplus of grandeur, a claustrophobic excess of nobility. Thus it is that the stylized language of official ceremony comes to be felt as parodic stylization, the discourse being shown *up* in the very process of being shown off; we are made to feel its limits as well as its loftiness. 'Parodic', here, should not give the wrong emphasis; Bakhtin does not use it to imply a crude travesty of the stylized language. Rather, as he puts it, 'parodied discourse, in an authentic prose image, can offer internal dialogic resistance to the parodying intentions' (Bakhtin 1981: 419). And this is surely what happens here, where the language is both genuinely impressive and stiflingly oppressive all at once. The passage is 'double-voiced' because *two* sets of intentions are at work in the single verse paragraph: the intentions of the lady, straightforwardly using this elevated style to express her sense of her own milieu, and the refracted intentions of the author, undermining the authority of the discourse in the very act of writing in it, exposing it as merely one among the many languages of social heteroglossia.

The issue of parody is worth pursuing, especially as we move a few lines further into the poem where a cynically debunking voice does indeed seem to enter it:

Above the antique mantle was displayed
As though a window gave upon the sylvan scene

The change of Philomel, by the barbarous king
So rudely forced; yet there the nightingale
Filled all the desert with inviolable voice
And still she cried, and still the world pursues,
'Jug Jug' to dirty ears.
And other withered stumps of time
Were told upon the walls; staring forms
Leaned out, leaning, hushing the room enclosed.

(*WL*, ll. 97–106)

The phrases 'antique mantle', 'sylvan scene' and 'rudely forced' rewrite
the rape of Philomel in the 'inviolable voice' of ceremonious, epic for-
mality that we have become accustomed to by now, but this style is then
brutally disrupted by the crudely sexualizing 'Jug Jug' of dirty ears. The
following line – 'other withered stumps of time' – sounds like direct
authorial discourse, turning harshly (but deservedly) upon the dignified,
'overwritten' style that the poet has been ventriloquizing from the
inside up to now. Yet the discourse which unmasks another discourse
in *The Waste Land* never has time to acquire an authority of its own,
authorial or otherwise; it, too, at once dwindles into an 'image of a
language', socially typical and (in Bakhtin's fine phrase) 'contested, con-
testable and contesting' (Bakhtin 1981: 332). The dry dismissiveness of
'withered stumps of time' is not direct authorial intervention, but rather
the first anticipatory trace in the text of a heteroglot discourse which
bursts forcefully upon us some thirty lines later:

When Lil's husband got demobbed, I said –
I didn't mince my words, I said to her myself,
HURRY UP PLEASE ITS TIME
Now Albert's coming back, make yourself a bit smart.
He'll want to know what you done with that money he gave you
To get yourself some teeth.

(*WL*, ll. 139–44)

A language capable of 'withering' the grand style of the opening of this
section now assumes the accents of working-class female vulgarity (as
Eliot sees it), of the unstoppable energies of lower-class gossip. 'That
one of the main subjects of human speech is discourse itself has not up
to now been sufficiently taken into consideration', claims Bakhtin
(1981: 355); and gossip, which consists in relaying to an audience the
words of others, would be a privileged genre for the Bakhtinian analysis
of 'discourse as the subject of discourse' (1981: 337). At any rate, the

transformation of the debunking discourse ('stumps of time') into a class- and gender-specific heteroglot dialect of its own illustrates a key Bakhtinian principle:

> where hybridization occurs, the language being used to illuminate another language . . . is reified to the point where it itself becomes an image of a language. The more broadly and deeply the device of hybridization is employed in a novel – since it occurs not with one but with several languages – the more reified becomes the represented and illuminating language itself.
>
> (Bakhtin 1981: 361)

The debunked thus succeeds in debunking its debunker – which would serve as an effective brief summary of the fate of Tiresias in 'The Fire Sermon'. Tiresias's grandly prophetic discourse – 'I Tiresias have fore-suffered all' – strives to make contemptible the modern love-making of the typist and her 'young man carbuncular' (l. 231). Yet the discourse of modernity, with its distinctive tones and objects (taxis, tinned food, gramophones), is sufficiently present in this passage to reify Tiresias's lofty authority into mere class snobbery, as when he describes the house agent's clerk as 'One of the low on whom assurance sits/As a silk hat on a Bradford millionaire' (ll. 233–4), or even into the shabby sexual voyeurism of a fetishist – 'Stockings, slippers, camisoles, and stays' (l. 227).

Heteroglossia in *The Waste Land* consistently undermines the claims to authority of any particular discourse. Almost every time we find ourselves confronted by a lofty discourse it turns out to be a Bakhtinian parodic stylization, reified into a bounded, discrete 'image of a language' by other styles and languages beyond its social ken. In this way, in 'The Burial of the Dead', the discourses of aristocracy (Marie), religious tradition ('Son of man') and romantic love (Wagner, the hyacinth girl) are all reified by being juxtaposed to the lower-middle-class vulgarity of 'Madame Sosostris, famous clairvoyante' and her spiritualist *demi-monde*.[4] Yet we must also note the presence of a distinct counter-impulse in the poem, an attempt to find some ultimate discourse of authority that would unify or transcend the many heteroglot fragments of which the text is composed. Bakhtin argues that 'every concrete utterance of a speaking subject serves as a point where centrifugal as well as centripetal forces are brought to bear', so that one must analyse the utterance as 'a contradiction-ridden, tension-filled unity of two embattled tendencies in the life of language' (Bakhtin 1981: 272); and this is no less true of that extended concrete utterance which is Eliot's *The Waste Land*.

Though heteroglossia – different voices, styles, genres – so productively enters the poem, we must also recall that crucial endnote where Eliot claims that Tiresias is 'the most important personage in the poem, *uniting* all the rest' (*CPP*, 78; emphasis added). I have suggested that Tiresias in fact cannot live up to his high Eliotic vocation but is (in a Bakhtinian metaphor) 'infected' by heteroglossia, but it is certainly an important fact about the text that the note *wants* him to be a monological voice of supreme, transhistorical authority, even if it cannot actually quite produce the goods when it comes to it. A more impressive attempt at a language of mastery and wisdom is provided by the Sanskrit of 'What the Thunder Said': *Datta, Dayadhvam, Damyata*, Shantih shantih shantih. This is a move from the 'centrifugal' to the 'centripetal' with a vengeance. The poem proceeds from the polyglot dispersion of the modern European languages to their ultimate monoglot linguistic roots, a language of Truth before the Fall into a Babel of mutually incomprehensible tongues. Though so many styles, voices and quotations enter the text, they are all, arguably, quelled by this formidable, monologic language of origins; *The Waste Land* lets heteroglossia in, it has been claimed, only forcibly to *expel* it again in its closing pages. Indeed, ultimately even Sanskrit may not be adequate to the poem's religious purposes. Since *no* human discourse is adequate to God or mystic vision or the Absolute, the poem in a sense aspires beyond language altogether, towards that 'heart of light, the silence', that moment of transcendental insight, of which nothing whatsoever can be said.[5]

At this point, however, we arrive at *The Waste Land*'s most remarkable paradox – and one which perhaps explains why the politics of this text has seemed so ambivalent during the seventy years since its composition. For a religious reading of the poem, God or the Absolute is an 'absent presence' in *The Waste Land*. Language can gesture towards this ultimate reality, but – smitten by original sin as all human things are – it can never deliver it up with any fullness. But this claim, startlingly, could also apply to Bakhtinian heteroglossia which, as 'Discourse in the Novel' insists several times, is also an absent presence even in the greatest novels. Dialogism in the novel can never be given in full, can never really be pinned down: it 'cannot fundamentally be dramatized or dramatically resolved (brought to an authentic end); it cannot ultimately be fitted into the frame of any manifest dialogue, into the frame of a mere conversation between persons' (Bakhtin 1981: 326).

Since novelistic prose 'grows organically out of a stratified and hetero-glot language' (1981: 326), a social heteroglossia which is a vast, anonymous, endless process of linguistic becoming and proliferation, dialogue in a novel 'is pregnant with an endless multitude of dialogic confrontations, which do not and cannot resolve it, and which, as it were, only locally (as one out of many possible dialogues) illustrate this endless, deep-lying dialogue of languages' (1981: 365). Devoted to a social heteroglossia which can never finally be given positive form, the novel itself comes to seem an absent presence in Bakhtin's prose. It has no substance or 'approach of its own, and therefore requires the help of other genres to reprocess reality; the novel itself has the appearance of being merely a syncretic unification of other seemingly primary verbal genres' (1981: 321). The greatest novelists, such as Rabelais, are those who most intensify one's sense of *absence*, that absence of an authoritative language which is the only way one can keep faith with the elemental, protean energies of heteroglossia. In Rabelais, truth

> reverberates only in the parodic and unmasking accents in which the lie is present. Truth is restored by reducing the lie to an absurdity, but truth itself does not seek words; she is afraid to entangle herself in the word, to soil herself in verbal pathos.
>
> (Bakhtin 1981: 309)

Every word of this last sentence of Bakhtin's could be applied directly to that *religious* truth, that 'heart of light, the silence', at which *The Waste Land* is aimed – a truth for which, in the long run, not even the Sanskrit of the Thunder is adequate. All language soils it. Exposing all words as lies, absurdities, sins, it none the less (or therefore) has no word of its own, and the poem can only make you feel its 'presence' by giving you a more intense awareness of its *absence*.

So we end up with two quite distinct, but equally convincing, terminologies for discussing what *The Waste Land* is ultimately about. First (the conventional reading), it is about God, religious faith, transcendental reality, which it must use all the possible varieties of human language to gesture at, while knowing that even the most authoritative of them will always fail to reach it. Second (the Bakhtinian approach), it is about social heteroglossia, a vast, unrepresentable process of language stratification which even all the diverse voices, styles and allusions of *The Waste Land* can only provide local instances of, mere illustrative gestures towards. God and heteroglossia, it seems, turn out to be the same thing (a claim which would be less shocking if we had space here to consider how Bakhtin's own religious convictions might have shaped his linguistic and literary theory). But even if they are, your choice of vocabulary clearly leads to a quite different overall assessment of Eliot's poem. If you choose the terminology of religious transcendence, then *The Waste Land* emerges as a politically conservative poem, seeking first to master the diversity of social languages in the name of a master discourse (Tiresias, Sanskrit) and then going even beyond these to a point or 'silence' of supreme authority. If, on the other hand, you employ a Bakhtinian terminology, then *The Waste Land* is a virtually revolutionary poem, opening the cultured upper-class salon to the heteroglot 'streets', overturning conventional literary language, parodically stylizing all would-be discourses of authority, religious or political. And this is, by and large, the way the critical history of the poem has divided: into conservative readings which emphasize the spiritual themes, and radical readings which emphasize Eliot's bold linguistic experimentation. The discovery that God and heteroglossia have the same structure (absent presence) does not constitute the last word in these interpretative disputes – for Bakhtin there is *never* a last word; the dialogue always goes on – but it does explain why the history of readings of the poem should have fissured in this dramatic manner.

IV

On the first page of 'Discourse in the Novel', Bakhtin argues that stylistics should concern itself with 'the great historical destinies of genres' rather than with individual poems, poets or movements (Bakhtin 1981: 259). This essay has been a compromise between these two approaches. Through a limited choice of examples analysed in some depth – 'Ode on a Grecian Urn', 'In a Station of the Metro', Eliot's early poems, *The Waste Land* itself – I have tried to evoke the fate of 'poetic discourse' across the last two centuries. I hope to have shown both that Bakhtin's theories of language are true – because social language is indeed dialogical and heteroglossic in the ways he describes – and that his account of the novel as the genre uniquely equipped to register and 'orchestrate' heteroglossia provides a satisfying approach to *The Waste Land*. Eliot's poem simply cannot be made sense of in the monological model of poetic discourse – unmediated authorial intention, unitary language, direct access to an unuttered object – which is perfectly adequate for 'Ode on a Grecian Urn' and for part of 'In a Station of the Metro'. 'Prufrock' and 'Portrait of a Lady' begin to make a break with the monological model of poetry. In them official literary language is relativized, but the heteroglossia of the streets, though it is thematically gestured towards, has not yet entered the poetry as a series of voices and styles in its own right. It is *The Waste Land* itself which makes that extraordinary break, becoming in the process a 'novel' in Bakhtin's terms.

On the whole, 'Discourse in the Novel' draws a very sharp distinction between poetry and the novel, poetic and novelistic (or prose) discourse. It does so for good tactical reasons, to highlight both the historical originality of the novel as a genre and the originality of its own contributions to stylistics. But the reader may have felt there is something irritatingly 'analogical' about my application of the Bakhtinian theory of the novel to Eliot's great poem, that I have consistently treated the latter 'as if' it were a novel, granted it honorary novel status, while ignoring the simple fact that, at the end of the day, it *is* a poem. I tried to address this anxiety (or frustration!) in my opening pages, suggesting that the logic of Bakhtinian theory is eventually to break down any rigid contrast between poetry and novel (some novels are 'unnovelistic', some poems are highly dialogical), and that there is a profound interbreeding of the two genres in modernist literary theory and practice. But it is true that 'Discourse in the Novel' is ultimately of limited help here. For a properly theorized justification for reading *The Waste Land* as a Bakhtinian novel we would have to turn to an earlier essay in *The Dialogical Imagination* on 'Epic and Novel'. Here Bakhtin proposes the striking idea of a 'novelization of literature', a 'novelization of other genres' (Bakhtin 1981: 39, 6), in eras when the novel becomes the dominant genre. In this process, the old fixed genres 'become more free and flexible, their language renews itself by incorporating extraliterary heteroglossia and the "novelistic" layers of literary language, they become dialogized, permeated with laughter, irony, humour, elements of self-parody':

> This occurred several times in the Hellenic period, again during the late Middle Ages and the Renaissance, but with special force and clarity beginning in the second half of the eighteenth century. In an era when the novel reigns supreme, almost all the remaining genres are to a greater or lesser extent 'novelized': drama (for example Ibsen, Hauptmann, the whole of Naturalist drama), epic poetry (for example, *Childe Harold* and especially Byron's *Don Juan*), even lyric poetry (as an extreme example, Heine's lyrical verse).
>
> (Bakhtin 1981: 5–6)

And it occurs again, exhilaratingly, in T.S. Eliot's *The Waste Land* in the early twentieth century.

SUPPLEMENT

TONY DAVIES: You mention the notorious note in which Eliot assigns to Tiresias a central, generative role in the poem, suggesting that the centrifugal forces in the text will not permit him to sustain that position with the authority and objectivity that the note wants to give him. What is your view of the notes in general? Do you read them as *part* of the text, integral to its dialogical variety? Or as themselves a (failed) totalizing reading, an extraneous discourse, attempting to impose order and objectivity from without?

TONY PINKNEY: Are notes a necessary part of a text? (I wonder how many readers of my essay dutifully turned up each footnote as it was signalled in the main text!) *The Waste Land* was originally published in 1922 without them (in literary periodicals in London and New York), and they were only added to the first publication in book form, also in 1922, at the publishers' request. They constitute, that is to say, part of the 'wrapping' or packaging of the published poem, forming a kind of container for it. But *The Waste Land* has a notably low opinion of wrappers and containers, whether these are the 'empty bottles, sandwich papers, / Silk handkerchiefs, cardboard boxes' evoked at the start of 'The Fire Sermon' or the 'tins' out of which the typist prepares her food. Notes, then, like these other wrappers, are junk, litter, debris, part of the 'waste' that encumbers a waste land.

Though the Notes do occasionally seek to assert a monological authority over the main text, as above all in the comments on Tiresias, they themselves, I think, belong to the genre of 'waste' or excess, a heteroglossic surplus which the mono-logic of the poem cannot manage. Thus for every apparently 'helpful' note – references to Jessie Weston or *The Golden Bough,* to the Tarot pack, or to Tiresias himself – we can find several bafflingly opaque and 'centrifugal' ones: allusions to *The Proposed Demolition of Nineteen City Churches* (complete with false publisher!), chunks solemnly quoted from the *Handbook of Birds of Eastern North America,* or notes which announce and erase themselves simultaneously ('I do not know the origin of the ballad from which these lines are taken'). As ever in this poem, heteroglossia and the monologic battle it out to an exhausted standstill.

TD: I have the impression that the early drafts of the poem were aiming at a higher degree of narrative and thematic coherence, at least within sections and perhaps overall. How much credit should go to Ezra Pound for the striking heteroglossia of the published text?

TP: Pound's role in producing the public text of *The Waste Land* can point us to a distinct limit in Bakhtinian theory. Just as some critics seek to fold all the voices of *The Waste Land* back into a single master consciousness, so Bakhtin, for all his celebration of many-styledness, tends to see all these styles as ultimately under the control of a governing authorial consciousness: his recurrent musical metaphor of 'orchestration' implies that there is a *conductor*, baton in hand, skilfully commanding the diverse stylistic 'instruments' of the text. Much contemporary theory, by contrast, has sought to do away with this notion of a masterful, lucid author governing the text from somewhere above or beyond it. Eliot, in the grip of an intense nervous breakdown as he worked upon *The Waste Land*, never was such a self-composed author in this sense, and Pound's interventions in the drafts show that, in practice as well as in theory, the production of powerful works is *not* dependent on the traditional category of the Author – a category which remains residually in place even in Bakhtin's path-breaking work.

TD: Your Eliot is a very European poet, an impression reinforced by the Europeanness of Bakhtin's concerns and references. Perhaps, again, with '*il miglior fabbro*' in mind, I'm inclined to ask: how *American* is *The Waste Land*?

TP: An 'American' *Waste Land*? One way of addressing this issue is to ask: who are the great figures of 'English literature' between, say, 1890 and 1930? A quite plausible answer is: three Americans, three Irishmen, and one Pole (James, Eliot, Pound; Wilde, Yeats, Joyce; Conrad). To see English literary and linguistic traditions from 'outside' seems, in this period, to be the condition for being able to experiment with and even revolutionize them. In the case of *The Waste Land*, in particular, it seems likely that its impressive Europe-wide range is a direct consequence of its American authorship. Eliot as an American expatriate seems to have been able to see Europe as a whole, from outside and (as it were) at arm's length, in a way that no native European could, immersed as she/he necessarily would be in a particular national cultural tradition. We do not, I suggest, have to choose between a European and an American *Waste Land*: the latter is rather the condition of possibility of the former.

Endpiece

TONY DAVIES

Surveying the mountain of commentary that Eliot's most famous poem has produced in the seventy years since it was first published, a reader is likely to be struck by the recurrence of two closely related motifs: the question of unity, and the problem of difficulty. Does *The Waste Land* have a single central meaning or 'plot'? and why is it so difficult to understand? The two are intimately connected because our model of understanding implies a capacity to organize the disparate data of perception into a unified *Gestalt*, a configurative pattern through which meaning is generated. To comprehend means, literally, to gather together, to shore fragments of experience against the ruins of disorder.

There may be ineluctable psychological, perhaps even neurological reasons for this. There are certainly very powerful cultural and ideological ones. Eliot, who brought a philosopher's as well as a poet's interests to the problem of understanding (his DPhil dissertation was on 'Knowledge and Experience' in the writings of the Oxford philosopher, F.H. Bradley), knew this well. When he wrote that the poet's mind is constantly 'amalgamating disparate experience' – falling in love, reading Spinoza, 'the noise of the typewriter or the smell of cooking' (*SE*, 287) – into unified wholes, he was merely reformulating the central *topos* of European aesthetics, its insistence that the work of art, however heterogeneous in its parts, must exhibit a central unity of structure and meaning in which every detail falls into place. And as Terry Eagleton has recently reminded us, that aesthetic predilection stands in metonymically for an unacknowledged politics, its rage for order betraying a deep unease with the chaotic heterogeneity of modernity (Eagleton 1990). Eliot's formulation of that rage, in his praise of Joyce's *Ulysses* for imposing order on 'the immense panorama of futility and chaos which is contemporary history', has already been noted, and is even more trenchantly paralleled by his older contemporary, Yeats: 'When I stand upon O'Connell Street Bridge in the half-light and notice that discordant architecture, all those electric signs, where modern heterogeneity has taken physical form, a vague hatred comes up out of my own dark' ('An introduction to my work' (1937), in Yeats 1961: 526). 'Hammer your thoughts into unity': Yeats's motto resonates across the opening decades of the century; and where the hammerings of Yeats, Joyce, Lawrence, Pound, Eliot, Woolf and others failed to deliver the unity they sought, the subsequent generations of critics who have flocked to their writings have laboured to complete the job for them. Here, by way of example, is one of Eliot's most assiduous commentators, indefatigably unearthing (or inventing) the connections *The Waste Land* itself fails to supply:

> The Tarot Fool, Mr. Eugenides, well born but fallen on evil days, is a cosmopolite . . . The very currents of the one-eyed merchant's trade hint that the joyous grape has shrivelled up in the waste land. The dried fertility symbol which he transports is equivalent to knowledge of the sacramental Grail mystery . . . He corresponds, moreover, to the chief actor in Frazer's account of the ritual 'ride of the beardless one' – which links Mr. Eugenides with the Hanged Man and even explains partly why Mr. Eugenides is unshaven. Either he has no beard to shave or he lets his beard flourish like the bearded Eastern patriarch of the Tarot – the man with three staves and hence a double for the Fisher King.
>
> (Grover Smith 1974: 87–8)

To the poem's anguished dyslexia ('I can connect/Nothing with nothing', ll. 301–2) this mode of commentary seems to reply: 'I can connect anything with absolutely anything else'. But its very determination to leave no loose end untied, no interpretative blank unfilled, no cryptographic 'correspondence' unexplained, testifies to the pitch of hermeneutic anxiety that *The Waste Land* can still produce.

For students faced with an assessed essay or examination paper, that anxiety, and the associated imperatives of coherence and comprehension, have a special and unavoidable urgency. But tempting though it must be in such situations to fall back on the reassuring, if illusory, solidity of a Grover Smith, it would be well to reflect that commentary of this kind, far from bringing the text closer, more vividly alive to the reader, actually effaces it, renders it obsolete. Pierre Macherey has called this sort of criticism 'rhapsody':

> The activity of the rhapsodist is twofold: he recites and he comments; he presents the work only in order to transpose it immediately . . . this simple repetition opens up within the work a possibility of indefinite proliferation. The critical process thus manages to expose a play of mirrors in the text: the book is shattered, dispersed among its reflections . . . Enveloped by the gaze of the critic, the work is merely the elaboration of a mirage. Entangled, folded into one another, the analysis and its object become strictly interchangeable.
>
> (Macherey 1978: 147–8)

'Indefinite proliferation', 'a play of mirrors in the text': these phrases anticipate some of the key formulations of the deconstructive enterprise; and Macherey's Marxist analysis of the compulsive doublings and redundancies of literary-critical commentary reminds us that the notorious 'difficulty' of modernist writing is only a special case of the difficulty of language in general. He quotes Foucault to the effect that commentary, in seeking to articulate what the text has not quite managed to say, betrays 'a strange attitude towards language'. To comment

> is to admit by definition an excess of the signified over the signifier; a necessary unformulated remainder of thought that language has left in the shade . . . but to comment also presupposes that this unspoken element slumbers within speech, and that, by a superabundance proper to the signifier, one may, in questioning it, give voice to a content that was not explicitly signified.
>
> (Macherey 1978: 148)

There are always things that remain unsaid; there is nothing that cannot be said. The impasse, Eliot's 'intolerable wrestle/With words and meanings' (*CPP*, 179), 'dooms us to an endless task that nothing can limit' (Macherey 1978: 148). Grover Smith's hectic determination to plug every interpretative mousehole ('Either he has no beard to shave or he lets his beard flourish . . .') raises as many problems as it solves, and each of his answers only poses a plethora of new questions. Between question and answer, poem and commentary, meaning, the elusive mouse, has escaped again.

Better, perhaps, to conclude that the mouse, the final definitive *explication de texte*, is not only elusive but illusory. Allon White, in his important (and lucid!) study of modernist difficulty, *The Uses of Obscurity*, argues that 'we cannot, even in principle, specify the "keys" or missing information which will enable us to find the meaning' of rebarbative modern texts.

> The obscurity of modernism is not susceptible to a simple decoding. It is usually not a matter of information suppressed or omitted which the critic can patiently recover . . . The formal, structural difficulties of a text, the kinds of de-formation that it uses, are inseparable from the way it produces significance . . . They are productive of meaning at the same time as (apparently) concealing meaning.
>
> (White 1981: 16)

For all the contributors to this collection, as for White, the complexities and obscurities of *The Waste Land* 'have positive functions' (White 1981: 16). For John Bowen, the poem's kaleidoscopic exposure of the waste and alienation of capitalist modernity, often seen as reactionary, can be given a radical, utopian turn, hinting at the possibility of a secular redemption of intolerable conditions. For Harriet Davidson, its very refusal of coherence, of the consoling infantilism of the Imaginary, betokens a commitment, painful and reluctant no doubt, to the Symbolic, the order of history, language, the struggle for identity and relationship. For Steve Ellis, the text's attempt to erase difficulty and impose a single authoritative reading, encapsulated in the famous Tiresias note, encounters the resistance of the reading process itself, with its inescapable plurality of performative encounters. For Tony Pinkney, the 'different voices' of the poem's early working title persist irreducibly in the published text, rooting it in the dialogical plurality and conflict of the actual. For all four, *The Waste Land* remains usable, pleasurable, instructive precisely to the extent that it remains 'difficult', incoherent, disorderly, resisting the classic status and interpretative security that literary criticism would like to confer.

But how 'difficult', in truth, *is The Waste Land* nowadays? Or rather, does not the question of the poem's celebrated difficulty have another, more political aspect? Reflecting some thirty years ago on the quandaries and contradictions facing a liberal academic engaged in the teaching of modern literature in a North American university, the critic Lionel Trilling wondered about the moral and political implications of confronting students, decent young men and women of impeccably liberal opinions and sensibilities, with a corpus of books so shockingly *illiberal*, so corrosively hostile in tone and substance to the progressive pieties and cherished values of the liberal establishment. The emptiness, horror and despair on display on every page of Kafka or Céline, the savage ironies of Conrad or Beckett, the hatred of the democratic decencies unleashed in the novels of Lawrence and the later poems of Yeats: what could it mean to encourage people not only to read these things but to admire, perhaps even to endorse them?

> How does one say that Lawrence is right in his great rage against the modern emotions, against the modern sense of life and ways of being, unless one speaks from the intimacies of one's own sense of life, and one's own wished-for way of being? How, except with the implication of personal judgement, does one say to students that Gide is perfectly accurate in his representation of the awful boredom and slow corruption of respectable life?
>
> (Trilling 1967: 23–4)

Trilling's answer was to conclude, glumly, that he and his fellow-teachers had devised all too effective a means of neutralizing the moral dilemmas and vulnerable exposures threatened by teaching modern authors, that the academic study of those very authors, in all its reverential and scrupulous attentiveness to form, language and other properly 'literary' concerns, tended inexorably to draw the sting of their seditious and oppositional energies, their potent capacity for shock and outrage. The naked, accusatory encounter of reader and text ('You! hypocrite lecteur! – mon semblable, – mon frere!') had the effect, in the academic setting, not of destabilizing or radicalizing the cosy assumptions of the reader but of transforming the text and its author into something even cosier and more innocuous: a classic (a process greatly assisted, in the case of *The Waste Land*, by Eliot's own later impersonation of an elderly publisher and conservative literary gent). Nowhere, Trilling argued, could that neutralizing tendency be more clearly seen than in the perennial academic protocols of assessment:

> 'Compare Yeats, Gide, Lawrence and Eliot in the use which they make of the theme of sexuality to criticize the deficiencies of modern culture. Support your statement by specific references to the work of each author. [Time: one hour.]' And the distressing thing about our examination questions is that they are not ridiculous, they make perfectly good sense – such good sense that the

young person who answers them can never again know the force and terror of what has been communicated to him by the works he is being examined on.

(Trilling 1966: 26)

There can be few students or teachers of literature to whom this depressing thought has not occurred; and it is undeniably true that the repetitive routines of teaching and examination can (perhaps must) reduce the thorniest of texts to the consistency of baby food, bland, painless and easily regurgitated. But Trilling's nostalgia for a pedagogy that will permit the student, like Browning's song-thrush, to 'recapture/The first fine careless rapture' of immediacy, the 'force and terror' of that primary encounter, is itself based on a myth, namely, that there can be such a thing as a direct, unmediated encounter between reader and text. Reading, like the texts with which it engages, belongs not to some elemental condition of primal appetites but to what Lacanians call the symbolic order, the world of social codes and meanings. It has to be learnt, and its strategies and rewards cannot be understood outside the wider purposes and expectations of particular cultures at certain moments of their history. Trilling's own assumption that the encounter with a text can communicate 'force and terror', and that this is something to be valued and desired, belongs to a specific historical tradition of modern aesthetics, an erotics of reading which can be traced from Burke's essay on the sublime, through the Romantic elevation of the 'life of sensations' above the 'life of thoughts', to Eliot's own ruminations on the vertiginous 'surrender' of the reader to the poem's dangerous enchantments.

If reading, far from 'coming naturally', is always constructed and informed by our cultural origins and destinations, and belongs as securely to the institutions of education as the teaching and criticism that seek, in Trilling's view, to alienate it from itself, then it follows that the vivid excitements and pleasures of modern writing (of any writing) will yield themselves not to the illusory pursuit of an original, Wordsworthian innocence and immediacy of perception, but to our willingness to confront our reading with something other than itself and thus, as the Formalists had it, to 'make it strange'. In this book, that 'something other' has been the writings of Benjamin, Lacan, Iser, Bakhtin, and the contributors' readings of them: a quartet diverse and incompatible enough, surely, to dispel any suspicion of orthodoxy, of theoretical canon-building. What the essays offer is not 'Great Theorists on *The Waste Land*', still less 'the Last Word on *The Waste Land*', but rather standpoints and perspectives from which the excitement, the singularity, the sheer strangeness of that extraordinary poem can be experienced and understood anew, and differently. That, if it is not to be simply another kind of academic examination-fodder, is what the engagement with 'theory' should mean.

Notes

Introduction

1 'Genuine poetry, seen in its proper role, performing for us what only it can perform, does contribute to the health of a culture. A first step toward the recovery of the health of our culture may well be the writing of a poetry that tells us the truth about ourselves in our present situation' (Brooks, in Tate 1967: 329). See also B. Rajan, 'The Overwhelming Question', in Tate (1967: 362–78).

2 Weston is not preoccupied with the linear narrative of the cults described in *From Ritual to Romance*: for example, 'It is the insistence on Life, Life continuous, and ever-renewing, which is the abiding characteristic of these cults' (Weston 1980: 8). The primary form of these rituals is the staging of the death and resurrection of vegetation. Eliot probably also took most of his knowledge of the Tarot pack from Weston (Weston 1980: 72–6); but see also Jay (1982) and Surette (1988).

3 Eliot's translation here christianizes the sentiment by relating it to Paul's words to the early congregations: 'And the peace of God, which passeth all understanding, shall keep your hearts and minds through Christ Jesus' (Philippians 4: 7). On this repetition, see Kearns (1987: 219–29), and Dwivedi (1982: 66–9).

4 The thunder-message occurs in a significantly different order from Eliot's: 'Control yourselves; give; be compassionate.' Eliot possibly stresses the aspect of control.

5 The poem's title alludes to Wordsworth's 'Ode: Intimations of Immortality from Recollections of Early Childhood' (1802–3; published in 1807),

and especially its joyous celebration of primal sympathies (ll. 169–87), exactly those sentiments that have been vanquished by the furtiveness of city life.

6 See Pound's comment in 1940 for the Gotham Book Mart's catalogue, *We Moderns* (New York): 'the immediate reception of it even by second-rate reviewers was due to the purely fortuitous publication of the notes, and not to the text itself. Liveright wanted a longer volume and the notes were the only available unpublished matter' (p. 24). See also Rainer (1989).

7 This has led to much opposition to the poem in that it is therefore elitist. John Carey has recently branded modernist principles as fashioning the 'exclusion of the masses, the defeat of their power, the removal of their literacy, the denial of their humanity' (Carey 1992: 21; see also 60, 65). For Terry Eagleton, in 1976, Eliot's classicism was well-timed: 'Confronted with world imperialist crisis, severe economic depression and intensifying working-class militancy, English society in the early years of Eliot's career as poet and critic stood in urgent ideological need of precisely the values his literary classicism encapsulated' (Eagleton 1976: 147). On Eliot's imperialist emphases, see David Trotter's 'Modernism and Empire: Reading *The Waste Land*', in MacCabe (1988: 143–53), and Svarny (1988: 174–207).

8 Most of the popular reviewers were doubtless more attuned to the Georgian poetry popularized by Edward Marsh's collections under that name (1911–12; 1913–15; 1916–17; 1918–19; 1920–22). Now condescended to, Marsh's high early hopes of a more dramatic and engaged idiom seem dated. There is an instructive comparison between *The Waste Land* and a Georgian poem of the last collection, published in November 1922: J.D.C. Pellow's 'After London'. Pellow's regular quatrains help convince us that there will be a reversion to a stable natural quiet, once the city has passed away:

> London Bridge is broken down;
>   Green is the grass on Ludgate Hill;
> I know a farmer in Camden Town
>   Killed a brock by Pentonville . . .
>
> Thinks I, while I smoke my pipe
>   Here beside the tumbling Fleet,
> Apples drop when they are ripe,
>   And when they drop are they most sweet.
>
> (ll. 1–4, 21–4)

See also Ross (1967: 222–55) and Simon (1975: 46–85).

9 For the fullest account, see Daniel H. Woodward, 'Notes on the Publishing History and Text of *The Waste Land*', *Papers of the Bibliographical Society of America* 58 (1964), 252–69, and Grant (1982, I: 17–30).

10 This had been the conclusion drawn of his earlier work. For example, see Babette Deutsch on 'Prufrock' – '[It] has the hall-marks of impressionism: remoteness from vulgar ethics and aesthetics, indifference to the strife of nations and classes . . .' (Grant 1982, I: 89) – or the unsigned review in the *Times Literary Supplement* (1917) – where he seems 'uninspired by any glimpse beyond [the self] and untouched by any genuine rush of feeling' (Grant 1982, I: 73).

11 But see the study by Gareth Reeves on Eliot's unconscious as well as overt Virgilian allusions (Reeves 1987).

12 Lyndall Gordon regards the process of Eliot's early career as one of a strenuous attempt to make sense of his intense spiritual life. The earliest motive behind the hoarding of fragments could well have been the desire to illustrate a 'spiritual journey from sin to salvation', to do with 'revelation and its aftermath' and the necessity of 'spurn[ing] the everyday world' (Gordon 1977: 86–7).

13 This is the common thread behind the verdicts of Hugh Kenner and F.O. Mathiesson. See Mathiesson's comments on the poem's 'musical organization' (Mathiesson 1947: 37) and Kenner's recognition of its 'new mode of poetic organization' near to a 'cinematic effect' (Kenner 1960: 156; see also Kenner 1972: 439–40, 442–4).

14 Gordon's view that Pound had actually been at sporadic work on some proto-*Waste Land* fragments as early as 1918 can be found in Gordon (1977: 106–9, 143–6).

15 This is one of the approaches taken by Robert Crawford in his study of Eliot's use of the city and savagery. See Crawford (1987: 3–5, 125–49).

16 J.R. Mulryne's note to this passage identifies a further relevance in the allusion: Babylon, in the Geneva Bible, used 'Babel' for both the Tower and Babylon, thus uniting the fall of a metropolis with linguistic confusion.

17 Eliot is clear in the Notes that he often worked this way with his allusions. See in the same note: 'The Man with Three Staves . . . I associate, quite arbitrarily, with the Fisher King himself'; or, to line 68: 'A phenomenon I have often noticed' (about Saint Mary Woolnoth's 'dead sound on the final stroke of nine'); or, to line 199: 'I do not know the origin of the ballad from which these lines are taken' – an example of his 'failed' annotation.

18 This lay behind Pound's advice to cut the first epigraph, from Conrad's *Heart of Darkness*, which Eliot had regarded as helpfully 'elucidative' (Pound 1951: 236).

19 See the pen-picture in 'The Age Demanded', where

> . . . his desire for survival,
> Faint in the most strenuous moods,
> Became an Olympian *apathein* [indifference]
> In the presence of selected perceptions.

(Pound 1933: 170)

20 In this, Eliot shows traces of his early interest in Symbolist poetry – see the influence of Jules Laforgue on his early work (Bergonzi 1978: 7–9, 24–5). One memorable formulation of Symbolism can be found in W.B. Yeats's 'The Symbolism of Poetry' (1900):

> All sounds, all colours, all forms, either because of their preordained energies or because of long association, evoke indefinable and yet precise emotions . . . [they exist] in a musical relation, a beautiful relation to one another, they become, as it were, one sound, one colour . . .
>
> (Yeats 1961: 157)

21 For example: 'The sentimental person, in whom a work of art arouses all sorts of emotions which have nothing to do with that work of art whatever, but are accidents of personal association, is an incomplete artist . . . [The fusion of disparate experiences creates] a new object which is no longer purely personal, because it is a work of art itself' (*SP*, 53).

22 See Wimsatt's 'The Intentional Fallacy' (first published in 1946) for propositions about the art-work without the artist:

> How are [we] to find out what the poet tried to do? If the poet succeeded in doing it, then the poem itself shows what he was trying to do . . . Judging a poem is like judging a pudding or a machine. One demands that it work. It is only because an artifact works that we infer the intention of the artificer . . . A poem can *be* only through its *meaning* . . .
>
> (Wimsatt 1970: 4).

23 One core problem concerns how we may regard and define the 'dramatic'. For Bernard Bergonzi, *The Waste Land* is a 'dramatic poem': 'the voices may weave in and out in an elusive way, but they have names and recognizable intonations and even, sometimes, personal identities' (Bergonzi 1986: 118). This may include some self-irony, but it implies no authorial voice. This is taken much further in Jonathan Bishop's reading, where the distrust of the direct communicative aspect of the words used in the poem (for the sake of erecting some ultimately non-verbal patterns) entails a disintegration of language (see Bishop 1985). See also Docherty (1987: 267–9) and, on the closing passage, Ellmann (1987: 107): 'It is as if the speaking subject had been "ruined" by the very fragments he had shored'.

1 The Politics of Redemption

1 Baudelaire, quoted by Walter Benjamin (1973: 119).
2 See for example Michel Foucault, 'What is Enlightenment?' in Paul

Rabinow (ed.), *The Foucault Reader* (Harmondsworth, 1984), 32–50.

3 'I think that from Baudelaire I learned first, a precedent for the poetic possibilities . . . of the more sordid aspects of the modern metropolis, of the possibilities of fusion between the sordidly realistic and the phantasmagoric, the possibility of the juxtaposition of the matter-of-fact and the fantastic.' T.S. Eliot, 'What Dante Means to Me', in *To Criticise the Critic and Other Writings* (1965). See also the essay on Baudelaire in Eliot (1951: 419–30).

4 Jürgen Habermas, *The Philosophical Discourse of Modernity* (Cambridge, 1987), 11–16.

5 Karl Marx, *The Eighteenth Brumaire of Louis Bonaparte* in David Fernbach (ed.), *Surveys From Exile* (Harmondsworth), 1973, 146.

6 See Julian Roberts, *Walter Benjamin* (1982), 197, 20.

7 The phrase is W.H. Auden's. See his 'September 1, 1939' in Edward Mendelson (ed.), *The English Auden* (1977), 245.

8 Angus Calder explains that silk handkerchiefs (*WL*, l. 178) were used as contraceptives in the period. See his *T.S. Eliot* (1987), 62.

9 Eliot was called a 'drunken helot' by Arthur Waugh in the *Quarterly Review*, reprinted in Grant (1982, I: 63–5).

10 F.R. Leavis, *New Bearings in English Poetry* (Harmondsworth, 1932), 81.

11 See respectively Leavis, *New Bearings*, 87; A.D. Moody, *Thomas Stearns Eliot: Poet* (Cambridge, 1979); Moretti (1983: 255).

12 Georg Lukács, 'The Ideology of Modernism' in *The Meaning of Contemporary Realism* (1963), 17–46.

13 Maud Ellmann, 'Eliot's Abjection' in John Fletcher and Andrew Benjamin (eds), *Abjection, Melancholia and Love: the Work of Julia Kristeva* (1990).

2 The Logic of Desire

1 Marianne DeKoven (1991) discusses the unresolved contradiction of modernism as a writing *sous-rature*.

2 See works by Spanos (1979), Jay (1983), Davidson (1985), Nevo (1985), Bedient (1986), Beehler (1987) and Brooker and Bentley (1990) for readings of Eliot through various deconstructive and poststructuralist paradigms which emphasize the absence and disruption in the poem.

3 For recent readings which rely on psychoanalytic mechanisms see Ross (1986) and Ellman (1987).

4 I am indebted to the many fine critical works on Lacan, some of which I quote below. I would send the English reader wanting more explication of his ideas to the work of Wilden (1968), Gallop (1982), Mitchell and Rose (1982), Muller and Richardson (1982), Schneiderman (1983), Bowie (1987), Dews (1987), Smith (1988) and Nancy and Lacoue-Labarthe (1992).

5 See Smith (1988: 70–5) for a good discussion of the unconscious in Lacan. Smith also provides an acute appreciation and critique of the subject in Lacan's system.

6 See Mitchell and Rose (1982) and Gallop (1982) for the feminist appropriation of Lacan's work.

7 In *The Waste Land: A Facsimile and Transcript of the Original Drafts* (Eliot 1971), these images are much clearer, particularly in the viciously satirical Fresca section, edited out of the published version of the poem.

8 In the Notes to the poem Eliot quotes F.H. Bradley's statement of solipsism in relation to this line, but in his doctoral dissertation of 1916 Eliot is at some pains to refute the possibility of solipsism, saying that the sense of self only comes with a sense of others. But Eliot is sympathetic with the prisons we imagine for ourselves.

9 See Cooper (1987) for a close analysis of class prejudice in the poem.

3 *The Waste Land* and the Reader's Response

1 A useful summary of Iser's model and his terminology (though without any application specifically to modern literature) can be found in Iser (1980).

2 See his reply to Norman Holland in the interview with Iser in *Diacritics* 10 (Summer 1980), 65, reprinted in Iser (1989: 54–5).

3 'Negativity' is a complex concept in Iser's work: as well as Iser (1978: 225–31), see the Introduction to Wolfgang Iser and Sandford Budick (eds), *Languages of the Unsayable: the Play of Negativity in Literature and Literary Theory* (New York, 1989), xi–xxi, and 'The Pattern of Negativity in Beckett's Prose' in Iser (1989: 140–51).

4 It is arguable that enough survives from the original drafts of *The Waste Land* to justify us in retaining the term 'a London poem' for the final version, in accordance with Hugh Kenner's discussion of the drafts. See 'The Urban Apocalypse' in A. Walton Litz (ed.), *Eliot in His Time: Essays on the Occasion of the Fiftieth Anniversary of The Waste Land* (Princeton, NJ, 1973), 27.

5 See also Iser (1989: 131–9) for further argument that Joyce's novel thematizes 'experienceability' itself.

6 See, for example, the essays on Joyce and Beckett referred to in note 3 above and in '*Ulysses* and the Reader' in Iser (1989).

7 That narrator and Stetson mirror one another might be underlined by the similarity of the latter's name to Eliot's own nickname (based on the duplication of his initials), 'Tsetse'. At the end of Section I of *The Waste Land*, then, we would have an anticipation of the famous meeting with the double in Section II of 'Little Gidding' (*CPP*, 193–4). The frequent identification of Stetson with Ezra Pound seems to have no justification whatever.

8 See the extract from his letter of 14 August 1923 to Ford Madox Ford, quoted in Valerie Eliot (*WLF*, 129).

9 See Ellis (1991: 33), where the points made in the present paragraph are substantiated in more detail.

10 Such a reading bears some resemblance to Iser's own discussion of Fielding's *Tom Jones*, where the presentation of 'the whole spectrum of human nature' exposes the severely restrictive nature of eighteenth-century regulatory norms on human behaviour. See Iser (1978: 198–202).

11 The Earl of Birkenhead, 'Fiery Particles', in David Pryce-Jones (ed.), *Evelyn Waugh and His World* (1973), 138. Acton's recital is fictionalized in the character of Anthony Blanche in Waugh's *Brideshead Revisited* (Harmondsworth, 1962), 42.

12 I.A. Richards, *Science and Poetry* (1926), 64–5. Eliot's objection to Richards's statement (which I return to later) is in his *The Use of Poetry and the Use of Criticism* (*UPUC*, 130).

13 For the importance of Richards's work to reader-response criticism see Freund (1987: 23–39).

14 See the interview with Eliot in the *Paris Review*, 21 (Spring–Summer 1959), 63–4, reprinted in Van Wyck Brooks (ed.), *Writers at Work: the Paris Review Interviews*, second series.

15 Quoted by Stephen Spender in 'Remembering Eliot', *Encounter*, April 1965, 4; reprinted in Tate (1967: 42). Spender suggests that the reply was 'not altogether . . . fair', given that Eliot's Notes to *The Waste Land* seem to encourage such interpretative questions.

4 *The Waste Land*, Dialogism and Poetic Discourse

1 In Dickens's novel (*Our Mutual Friend*, Book 1, chapter 16) the foundling Sloppy is described as 'a beautiful reader of a newspaper. He do the police in different voices'. Some critics have traced the mimicry and ventriloquism of the poem to a 'Sloppy', a single voice and presiding consciousness. For reasons elaborated in this essay, I disagree with that claim.

2 T.E. Hulme, 'Romanticism and Classicism' in Herbert Read (1960: 134); F.S. Flint, 'Imagisme' in Jones (1972: 129).

3 For an excellent brief account of Russian Formalism see Ann Jefferson, 'Russian Formalism' in Jefferson and Robey (1986: 24–45).

4 For a detailed account of the motif of aristocracy in the poem, all the way from Marie and her archduke to the 'broken Coriolanus' of its last page, see my 'Aristocracy in *The Waste Land*' in Cookson and Loughrey (1988: 21–30).

5 Calvin Bedient has produced a book-length reading of the poem along these lines in his *He Do The Police In Different Voices: 'The Waste Land' and its Protagonist* (1986). This energetic interpretation, which makes much use of

Bakhtin's work, relies on the hypothesis that 'there is a single presiding consciousness in the poem, that of a poet-protagonist who is "dramatizing" (for want of a more exact word) the history of his own religious awakening' (1986: ix). This hypothesis seems to me quite unnecessary.

References

Unless otherwise stated, place of publication is London.

Bakhtin, Mikhail (1968) *Rabelais and His World*. Cambridge, MA.

Bakhtin, Mikhail (1981) *The Dialogic Imagination: Four Essays*, ed. Michael Holquist and trans. Caryl Emerson and Michael Holquist. Austin, TX and London.

Bedient, Calvin (1986) *He Do The Police In Different Voices: 'The Waste Land' and its Protagonist*. Chicago.

Beehler, Michael (1987) *T.S. Eliot, Wallace Stevens, and the Discourses of Difference*. Baton Rouge, LA.

Benjamin, Walter (1970) *Illuminations*.

Benjamin, Walter (1973) *Charles Baudelaire: A Lyric Poet in the Era of High Capitalism*.

Bennett, Tony (1979) *Formalism and Marxism*.

Bergonzi, Bernard (1978) *T.S. Eliot*, 2nd edn (1st edn 1972).

Bergonzi, Bernard (1986) *The Myth of Modernism and Twentieth Century Literature*. Brighton.

Bishop, Jonathan (1985) A handful of words: The credibility of language, in *The Waste Land*, *Texas Studies in Literature and Language*, 27: 154–77.

Bloch, Ernst and others (1977) *Aesthetics and Politics*.

Bowie, Malcolm (1987) *Freud, Proust and Lacan: Theory as Fiction*. Cambridge.

Brooker, Jewel Spears and Bentley, Joseph (1990) *Reading 'The Waste Land': Modernism and the Limits of Interpretation*. Amherst, MA.

Carey, John (1992) *The Intellectuals and the Masses: Pride and Prejudice among the Literary Intelligentsia, 1880–1939*.

Cookson, Linda and Loughrey, Brian (eds) (1988) *Critical Essays on 'The Waste Land'*.

Cooper, John Xiros (1987) *T.S. Eliot and the Politics of Voice: The Argument of 'The Waste Land'*. Ann Arbor, MI and London.

Crawford, Robert (1987) *The Savage and the City in the Work of T.S. Eliot*. Oxford.

Culler, Jonathan (1983) *On Deconstruction: Theory and Criticism After Structuralism*.

Davidson, Harriet (1985) *T.S. Eliot and Hermeneutics: Absence and Interpretation in 'The Waste Land'*. Baton Rouge, LA.

DeKoven, Marianne (1991) *Rich and Strange: Gender, History and Modernism*. Princeton, NJ.

Dews, Peter (1987) *Logics of Disintegration: Poststructural Thought and the Claims of Critical Theory*.

Dickens, Charles (1971) *Our Mutual Friend*, ed. Stephen Gill. Harmondsworth.

Docherty, Thomas (1987) *On Modern Authority: The Theory and Condition of Writing, 1500 to the Present Day*. Brighton.

Dwivedi, A.N. (1982) *T.S. Eliot's Major Poems: An Indian Interpretation*. Salzburg.

Eagleton, Terry (1976) *Criticism and Ideology*.

Eagleton, Terry (1990) *The Ideology of the Aesthetic*. Oxford.

Easthope, Anthony (1983) The Waste Land as a dramatic monologue, *English Studies* 4: 330–44.

Eliot, T.S. (1920) *The Sacred Wood: Essays on Poetry and Criticism*.

Eliot, T.S. (1933) *The Use of Poetry and the Use of Criticism* (reprinted in 1964).

Eliot, T.S. (1951) *Selected Essays*, 3rd enlarged edn.

Eliot, T.S. (1957) *On Poetry and Poets*.

Eliot, T.S. (1969) *Complete Poems and Plays*.

Eliot, T.S. (1975) *Selected Prose of T.S. Eliot*, ed. Frank Kermode.

Eliot, T.S. (1988) *The Letters of T.S. Eliot, Volume 1 1898–1922*. New York and London.

Eliot, Valerie (ed.) (1971) *The Waste Land: A Facsimile and Transcript of the Original Drafts*.

Ellis, Steve (1991) *The English Eliot: Design Language and Landscape in Four Quartets*.

Ellmann, Maud (1987) *The Poetics of Impersonality: T.S Eliot and Ezra Pound*. Brighton.

Ellman, Maud (1990) Eliot's abjection, in John Fletcher and Andrew Benjamin (eds), *Abjection, Melancholia and Love: The Work of Julia Kristeva*.

Fish, Stanley (1981) Why no-one's afraid of Wolfgang Iser, *Diacritics*, 11: 2–13.

Freud, Sigmund (1953) *The Standard Edition of the Complete Psychological Works of Sigmund Freud*, ed. J. Strachey, 24 vols.

Freund, Elizabeth (1987) *The Return of the Reader: Reader-Response Criticism*.

Gallop, Jane (1982) *The Daughter's Seduction: Feminism and Psychoanalysis*. Ithaca, NY.

Gardner, Helen (1949) *The Art of T.S. Eliot.*

Gordon, Lyndall (1977) *Eliot's Early Years.* Oxford.

Grant, Michael (1982) *T.S. Eliot: The Critical Heritage*, 2 vols.

Holub, Robert C. (1984) *Reception Theory: A Critical Introduction.*

Hulme, T.E. (1924) *Speculations: Essays on Humanism and the Philosophy of Art.*

Iser, Wolfgang (1974) *The Implied Reader: Patterns of Communication in Prose Fiction from Bunyan to Beckett.* Baltimore, MD.

Iser, Wolfgang (1978) *The Act of Reading: A Theory of Aesthetic Response.*

Iser, Wolfgang (1980) Interaction between text and reader, in Susan R. Suleiman and Inge Crosman (eds), *The Reader in the Text: Essays on Audience and Interpretation.* Princeton, NJ. (Reprinted in Iser (1989)).

Iser, Wolfgang (1981) Talk like whales, *Diacritics*, 11: 82–7.

Iser, Wolfgang (1989) *Prospecting: From Reader Response to Literary Anthropology.* Baltimore, MD.

Jameson, Fredric (1971) *Marxism and Form.*

Jameson, Fredric (1981) *The Political Unconscious: Narrative as a Socially Symbolic Act.*

Jay, Gregory (1982) Eliot's Poetics and the Fisher King, *Yeats–Eliot Review*, 7: 28–35.

Jay, Gregory (1983) *T.S. Eliot and the Poetics of Literary History.* Baton Rouge, LA.

Jefferson, Ann and Robey, David (eds) (1986) *Modern Literary Theory: A Comparative Introduction.*

Jones, Peter (ed.) (1972) *Imagist Poetry.* Harmondsworth.

Kearns, Cleo McNally (1987) *T.S. Eliot and Indic Traditions: A Study in Poetry and Belief.* Cambridge.

Kenner, Hugh (1960) *The Invisible Poet: T.S. Eliot.*

Kenner, Hugh (1972) *The Pound Era: The Age of Ezra Pound, T.S. Eliot, James Joyce and Wyndham Lewis.*

Kyd, Thomas (1985) *The Spanish Tragedy*, ed. J.R. Mulryne.

Lacan, Jacques (1977) *Ecrits: A Selection.* New York.

Leavis, F.R. (1932) *New Bearings in English Poetry: A Study of the Contemporary Situation.*

MacCabe, Colin (ed.) (1988) *New Futures for English.* Manchester.

Macherey, Pierre (1978) *A Theory of Literary Production*, trans. Geoffrey Wall.

Matthiesson, F.O. (1947) *The Achievement of T.S. Eliot: An Essay on the Nature of Poetry*, 2nd edn. New York (1st edn 1935).

Mitchell, Juliet and Rose, Jacqueline (eds) (1982) *Feminine Sexuality: Jacques Lacan and the 'Ecole Freudienne'.*

Moretti, Franco (1983) *Signs Taken for Wonders.*

Muller, John P. and Richardson, William J. (1982) *Lacan and Language: A Reader's Guide to Ecrits.* New York.

Nancy, Jean-Luc and Lacoue-Labarthe, Philippe (1992) *The Title of the Letter: A Reading of Lacan*, trans. François Raffoul and David Pettigrew. Albany, NY.

Nevo, Ruth (1982) *The Waste Land*: The ur-text of deconstruction, *New Literary History*, 13: 453–61.

Pinkney, Tony (1984) *Women in the Poetry of T.S. Eliot: A Psychoanalytic Approach*.

Pinkney, Tony (1988) Aristocracy in *The Waste Land*, in Linda Cookson and Brian Loughrey (eds), *Critical Essays on 'The Waste Land'*.

Pound, Ezra (1933) *Selected Poems*. ed. T.S. Eliot (1st edn 1928).

Pound, Ezra (1951) *The Letters of Ezra Pound*, ed. D. Paige.

Pound, Ezra (1954) *Literary Essays of Ezra Pound*.

Rainer, Lawrence (1989) The price of modernism: Reconsidering the publication of *The Waste Land*, *Critical Quarterly*, 31: 21–47.

Read, Herbert (ed.) (1960) *Speculations: Essays on Humanism and the Philosophy of Arts*.

Reeves, Gareth (1987) *The Waste Land* and the *Aeneid*, *Modern Language Review*, 82: 555–72.

Ross, Andrew (1986) *Failures of Modernism: Symptoms of American Poetry*. New York.

Ross, Robert H. (1967) *The Georgian Revolt: Rise and Fall of a Poetic Ideal, 1910–22* (1st edn 1965).

Schneiderman, Stuart (1983) *Jacques Lacan: The Death of an Intellectual Hero*. Cambridge, MA.

Sharpe, Tony (1991) *T.S. Eliot: a Literary Life*.

Simon, Myron (1975) *The Georgian Poetic*. Berkeley CA.

Smith, Grover (1974) *T.S. Eliot's Poetry and Plays*, 2nd edn. Chicago (1st edn 1956).

Smith, Grover (1983) *'The Waste Land'*.

Smith, Paul (1988) *Discerning the Subject*. Minneapolis, MN.

Spanos, William (1979) Repetition in *The Waste Land*: A phenomenological de-struction, *Boundary 2*, 8: 225–85.

Stead, C.K. (1986) *Pound, Yeats, Eliot and the Modernist Movement*.

Stock, Noel (1970) *The Life of Ezra Pound*. New York.

Surette, Leon (1988) *The Waste Land* and Jessie Weston: A reassessment, *Twentieth Century Literature*, 34: 223–44.

Svarny, Erik (1988) *'The Men of 1914': T.S. Eliot and Early Modernism*. Milton Keynes.

Tate, Allen (ed.) (1967) *T.S. Eliot: The Man and his Work*. Harmondsworth (1st edn 1966).

Trilling, Lionel (1966) *Beyond Culture*.

Volosinov, Valentin (1986) *Marxism and the Philosophy of Language*, trans. L. Matejka and I.R. Titunik.

Waugh, Patricia (1992) *Practising Postmodernism, Reading Modernism*.

Weston, Jessie L. (1980) *From Ritual to Romance*. Bath (first published 1920, Cambridge).

White, Allon (1981) *The Uses of Obscurity*.

Wilden, Anthony, trans. (1968) Jacques Lacan, *The Language of the Self: The Function of Language in Psychoanalysis*. New York.

Wimsatt, W.K. (1970) *The Verbal Icon: Studies in the Meaning of Poetry*. New York (first published 1964).

Wolin, Richard (1982) *Walter Benjamin, An Aesthetic of Redemption*. New York.

Yeats, W.B. (1961) *Essays and Introductions*.

Further Reading

1 The Politics of Redemption

Walter Benjamin, *Charles Baudelaire: A Lyric Poet in the Era of High Capitalism* (1973).
   Benjamin's unfinished masterpiece, full of insights into modernity and modern literature. The essay 'Some Motifs in Baudelaire' is particularly relevant to *The Waste Land*.

Ernst Bloch and others, *Aesthetics and Politics* (1977).
   Some of the most important debates on the politics of modernism, including contributions by Benjamin, Brecht, Lukács and others. The debate between Benjamin and Adorno defines very well two different left-wing arguments.

Maud Ellman, 'Eliot's abjection', in John Fletcher and Andrew Benjamin (eds), *Abjection, Melancholia and Love: The Work of Julia Kristeva* (1990).
   Probably the best modern reading of *The Waste Land*.

Fredric Jameson, *Marxism and Form* (Princeton, 1971).
   Still perhaps the best introduction to 'western Marxism', by a critic of major importance.

Franco Moretti, 'From *The Waste Land* to the artificial paradise', in *Signs Taken for Wonders* (1983).
   A hostile account of the poem, placed in the history of twentieth-century capitalist society.

2 The Logic of Desire

Stuart Schneiderman, *Jacques Lacan: Death of an Intellectual Hero* (Cambridge, MA, 1983).

Schneiderman writes a lively and engaging narrative about Lacan's career and clearly explains the revolutionary nature of his ideas for psychoanalysis.

Shoshana Felman, *Jacques Lacan and the Adventure of Insight* (1987).

Another important and more or less accessible work on Lacan, especially the wonderful and much anthologized chapter 'Psychoanalysis and education: Teaching terminable and interminable'. Both Schneiderman and Felman begin as professors of literature, and their work is especially helpful for literary readers.

Peter Dews, *Logics of Disintegration: Poststructural Thought and the Claims of Critical Theory* (1987).

A good resource for understanding Lacan's philosophical background and his connection to other contemporary thinkers. The two chapters on Lacan give an acute and surprisingly sympathetic reading of Lacan from a political perspective.

Anthony Wilden, *The Language of the Self: The Function of Language in Psychoanalysis* (New York, 1968).

A demanding but extremely important work on Lacan from a more strictly psychoanalytic perspective by his American translator, Wilden's book gives detailed explanations of many of Lacan's most difficult concepts.

3 *The Waste Land* and the Reader's Response

Jonathan Culler, *On Deconstruction: Theory and Criticism after Structuralism* (1983).

Includes a brief and not altogether sympathetic appraisal of Iser's work.

Stanley Fish, 'Why no one's afraid of Wolfgang Iser', *Diacritics*, 11 (Spring 1981), 2–13.

The best-known attack on Iser, in which Fish argues that literary texts have no inherent and objective theme-and-horizon structure, but that this too, is a construction of the individual reader's response and will differ from reader to reader.

Robert C. Holub, *Reception Theory: A Critical Introduction* (1984).

Contains an excellent general account of Iser's work.

Wolfgang Iser, *The Implied Reader: Patterns of Communication in Prose Fiction from Bunyan to Beckett* (Baltimore, MD, 1974).

This and the following item are two seminal works out of which Iser's model in *The Act of Reading* develops.

Wolfgang Iser, 'Indeterminacy and the reader's response in prose fiction', in J. Hillis Miller (ed.), *Aspects of Narrative* (New York, 1971); reprinted in Iser (1989: 3–30).
See previous item.

Wolfgang Iser, 'Talk like whales', *Diacritics*, 11 (Fall 1981), 82–7.
Iser's reply to Fish's attack (see above).

Jane P. Tompkins (ed.), *Reader-Response Criticism: From Formalism to Post-Structuralism* (Baltimore, MD, 1980).
A collection of extracts from the work of leading theorists in the field of readership, including Fish, Culler, Holland and Iser, part of whose *The Implied Reader* is included. There are useful introductory and concluding essays by the editor.

4 *The Waste Land*, Dialogism and Poetic Discourse

Calvin Bedient, *'He Do The Police In Different Voices': 'The Waste Land' and its Protagonist* (Chicago, 1986).
A powerful recent study of Eliot's poem, bringing a variety of critical perspectives to bear upon it. However, devoting 220 academic pages to Eliot's twenty-page text does mean that the commentary becomes rather remorseless at times.

Maud Ellman, *The Poetics of Impersonality: T.S. Eliot and Ezra Pound* (Brighton, 1987).
A sophisticated study of one of the central concepts of modernist poetics, which contains some subtle readings of Eliot's key poems.

Ken Hirschkop and David Shepherd (eds), *Bakhtin and Cultural Theory* (Manchester, 1989).
A bit more demanding than Holquist or Lodge (see below), this collection explores the enormous impact Bakhtin's work has had on literary and cultural thinking over the last decade. Both this and the Holquist volume contain very detailed and helpful Bibliographies.

Michael Holquist, *Dialogism: Bakhtin and His World* (1990).
Probably the best general introduction to Bakhtin, lucid and accessible on the theoretical side, and containing readings of Mary Shelley's *Frankenstein*, Scott Fitzgerald's *The Great Gatsby* and other texts.

David Lodge, *After Bakhtin: Essays on Fiction and Criticism* (1990).
Lodge has long been one of the most lucid expositors of theory and the most

sensitive commentators on fiction. This book combines both characteristic strengths.

Tony Pinkney, *Women in the Poetry of T.S. Eliot: A Psychoanalytic Approach* (1984).

Uses the psychoanalysis of Melanie Klein and D.W. Winnicott to read Eliot's work in the light of Sweeney's claim, in *Sweeney Agonistes*, that 'Any man has to, wants to, needs to/Once in a lifetime do a girl in'.

Index